DAILY SPELLING TEASERS

AGES 5–7

SUE GRAVES

CREDITS

Author
Sue Graves

Illustrations
Nick Diggory

Development Editor
Kate Pedlar

Series Designer
Anna Oliwa

Project Editor
Fabia Lewis

Designer
Mike Brain Graphic Design
Limited, Oxford

Text © Sue Graves
© 2008 Scholastic Ltd

Designed using Adobe InDesign

Published by Scholastic Ltd
Villiers House, Clarendon Avenue,
Leamington Spa, Warwickshire CV32 5PR

www.scholastic.co.uk

Printed by Bell and Bain Ltd

1 2 3 4 5 6 7 8 9   8 9 0 1 2 3 4 5 6 7

British Library Cataloguing-in-Publication Data
A catalogue record for this book is available from the
British Library.

ISBN 978-1407-10018-0

CONTENTS

DAILY SPELLING TEASERS FOR AGES 5–7

WHAT IS *DAILY SPELLING TEASERS*?

Daily Spelling Teasers 5–7 is a collection of over 170 spelling activities for everyday use. The activities teach patterns that can help children to learn how to spell high frequency words.

The spelling teasers include word games, puzzles, rhymes and story extracts. The ideas are designed to be used flexibly, and many can be easily adapted to reflect children's particular interests or to make cross-curricular links. In addition, most of the activities can be easily differentiated to cater for differing levels of ability within a class group.

HOW IS IT ORGANISED?

It is widely accepted that children learn in different ways. Teachers need to use a range of teaching styles and materials to ensure that all children are given the opportunity to learn.

The spelling teasers have therefore been grouped into four chapters, each focusing on different learning styles, thus providing a multi-sensory approach to learning:

1. Visual (seeing)
2. Auditory (hearing)
3. Tactile (touching)
4. Kinaesthetic (moving)

WHAT DOES EACH SPELLING TEASER CONTAIN?

Each spelling teaser focuses on a different aspect of word level work, such as spelling 'CVC' words and extending vocabulary through utilising topics such as 'animals'. The following information is also included within each activity:

Objective: This refers to the desired literacy skill to be developed.

Learning link: Where other learning styles feature in an activity, these are listed in this section.

Organisation: This gives information about the desired class arrangement for the activity, such as whole-class, pair or group work. However, many of the activities can be easily adapted to suit different circumstances.

Resources: A list of any items or photocopiable resources needed to carry out the activity is provided. This includes any items that need to be prepared in advance of the lesson.

What to do: This section provides brief instructions for carrying out the task. Where possible, these have been directed at the children themselves.

Now try this: At the end of each spelling teaser, suggestions have been given for how to extend learning in that particular activity in future lessons.

Answers: Answers are given, where appropriate.

HOW SHOULD THEY BE USED?

The spelling teasers are designed to provide ideas for ten-minute activities which should help to develop children's spelling skills. Some activities are to be adult-led (by a teacher or teaching assistant). However, in many cases, the activities are ideal for self-directed learning by the children themselves.

WHEN SHOULD THEY BE USED?

The spelling teasers can be used at any time throughout the school day, for example, to change the pace of a lesson; to reinforce specific spelling patterns; as a form of Brain Gym® or to encourage children to think independently.

Whenever you decide to use the spelling teasers always remember that learning to spell should be fun.

FLASH SOUNDS

OBJECTIVE: to read letter sounds a–z
LEARNING LINK: auditory
ORGANISATION: whole class
RESOURCES: a set of large single-letter flash cards (lower-case letters only) shuffled and with no picture cues

WHAT TO DO
- The teacher will show you a flash card.
- Remember to say the letter sound only – not the letter name.
- Say the letter sound aloud.
- If you are correct, the card will be placed to one side.
- If you are incorrect, the card will be placed at the back of the pile.

NOW TRY THIS
Shuffle the cards and see how fast you can say each letter sound. Repeat the activity and try to beat your time!

TRICKY LETTERS GAME

OBJECTIVE: to write letters b, d, p, q correctly
LEARNING LINK: auditory, tactile
ORGANISATION: groups of four (teacher/adult-led)
RESOURCES: eight laminated picture cards with a word written under each picture, but with the initial letter missing: 'bath', 'piano', 'dinosaur', 'queen', 'ball', 'quarter', 'pirate', 'duck'; dry-wipe markers, for each group

__ath

WHAT TO DO
- Look at one picture card.
- When asked, say the word.
- Write the missing letter in the space, using a dry-wipe marker.
- If you write the letter correctly, score a point.
- Repeat until all the cards have been used.
- The winner is the child with the most points.

NOW TRY THIS
Clean the writing from the pictures. Place the pictures face down on the table. Take turns to find two cards with matching first letter sounds. If a match is found, write in the missing letter and keep the cards. If the cards do not match, return them to the table. The winner is the child with the most pairs.

LETTER CARDS GAME

OBJECTIVE: to identify initial phonemes in words
LEARNING LINK: auditory, tactile
ORGANISATION: small groups
RESOURCES: sets of letter cards, for each group

WHAT TO DO
- Place the letter cards face down on a table.
- On your go, turn the cards over one at a time, and say the letter sound.
- Now think of a word that begins with that sound.
- If you are correct, keep the card.
- If incorrect, return the card to the table.
- The winner is the child with the most cards.

NOW TRY THIS
Play the game again, but this time, say and spell a word for each letter card. If you are correct, keep the card and score two points. The winner is the child who has the most points.

PICTURE CLUE GAME 1

OBJECTIVE: to identify initial phonemes in CVC words
LEARNING LINK: auditory
ORGANISATION: small groups
RESOURCES: a stack of 20 picture cards (CVC words only) for each group

dog

hat

bin

WHAT TO DO

- Turn over one card and look at it.
- Say what the picture shows, for example, *dog*. Then say the first letter sound *d* aloud.
- If you are correct you can keep that card.
- Now turn over a card for a different child in your group. They must say what the picture shows and then say the first letter sound aloud.
- If they are correct, give them the card.
- If they are incorrect, place the card at the back of the pile.
- The winner is the child with the most cards.

NOW TRY THIS

Play again, but this time, cover the cards so that only the pictures can be seen. When you hear a first letter sound you should point to the correct picture.

MIX AND MATCH

OBJECTIVE: to identify initial phonemes in words
LEARNING LINK: kinaesthetic
ORGANISATION: individual
RESOURCES: five pairs of picture cards (each pair has pictures with matching initial sounds, for example, pair 1 could be 'sock' and 'sun') for each child.

WHAT TO DO

- Shuffle the cards.
- Spread them out, face up, on the table.
- Look at each picture carefully. Match pairs of cards where the first letter sounds are the same.
- At the end of the session, check with the teacher that the pairs are correct.
- Practise the initial sounds of any wrongly matched pairs.

NOW TRY THIS

Use picture cards with items that have matching first consonant clusters, such as '*sc*arf' and '*sc*ales'; '*bl*ue' and '*bl*ack'.

ODD ONE OUT

OBJECTIVE: to identify initial phonemes in words
LEARNING LINK: auditory, tactile
ORGANISATION: small groups
RESOURCES: one tray; five sets of three items, for each group. Use items that are readily available in the classroom. Within each set of three items ensure only two begin with matching initial sounds, for example, '*pen*', '*pencil*', '*book*'

WHAT TO DO

- Look at the three items on the tray.
- Find the item that has a different first letter sound from the other two.
- Ask the others to say if you are right or not.
- As a group, practise saying the first letter sound for each item on the tray.
- The teacher will change the items on the tray.
- Repeat the activity.

NOW TRY THIS

1. Play the game again but this time, use five items. Who can spot the odd one out the fastest?
2. This time, find items with a different end sound from the other four.

PS AND QS GAME

OBJECTIVE: to hear and identify initial phonemes in words

LEARNING LINK: auditory, tactile

ORGANISATION: small groups (teacher/adult-led)

RESOURCES: individual letter cards showing 'p' and 'q', for each child

WHAT TO DO

● Each child in the group has a pair of letter cards – 'p' and 'q'.

● The adult says a word beginning with either 'p' or 'q', such as *park* or *queen*. Remember that 'q' usually has the letter 'u' with it!

● Hold up the correct first sound for each word the adult says.

● Score one point for each correct letter card.

● The winner is the child with the most points.

NOW TRY THIS

Play the game again, but this time the adult will add some red herrings (words beginning with 't'). If you hold up a card for a 't' word, you lose a point. The winner is the player with the most points.

PICTURE CLUE GAME 2

OBJECTIVE: to identify final phonemes in CVC words

LEARNING LINK: auditory

ORGANISATION: small groups

RESOURCES: a set of 20 picture cards (as for 'Picture clue game 1') for each group

WHAT TO DO

● Turn over one card from your stack and look at it.

● Say what the picture shows, for example, *hat*. Say the end letter sound *t*.

● Now turn over a card for a different child in your group. They must say what the picture shows and say the end sound.

● If they are correct, give them the card.

● If they are incorrect, place the card at the back of the pile.

● The winner is the child with the most cards.

NOW TRY THIS

Play again, but this time, cover the cards so that only the pictures can be seen. Point to the correct picture when you hear the end sound only.

AM I RIGHT?

OBJECTIVE: to identify initial and final phonemes in CVC words

LEARNING LINK: auditory

ORGANISATION: whole class

RESOURCES: prepared large picture cards of single items (write the initial sound and the final sound underneath each item; place a dash to show the position of the missing medial sound); small pieces of card with double-sided sticky tape on the back (these are for covering the CVC word at the bottom of each picture)

WHAT TO DO

● Look at the picture card, shown with the answer covered up.

● The teacher will say the first letter sound for the word. (Listen carefully as the teacher may say the wrong sound.)

● The teacher will ask whether you heard the correct letter sound.

● If you heard a mistake, tell the teacher the correct sound.

● Remove the sticky tape to reveal the right sound. Who was right?

● Now repeat the activity, but this time, listen for end letter sounds.

NOW TRY THIS

Listen for the vowel sound in the middle of the word.

CODE CRACKER

OBJECTIVE: to discriminate and segment all three phonemes in CVC words
LEARNING LINK: auditory
ORGANISATION: small groups
RESOURCES: a large whiteboard (write 'a b c d e f g' on the board and the numbers '1'–'7' below each corresponding letter; write a series of words in code on the board, for example, '214' for 'bad'); paper and pencils, for each group

a b c d
1 2 3 4

214 = bad

WHAT TO DO
● Use the code to find the words written as numbers on the board.
● Make up a new word using the code.
● Take turns to read out your code for the others to crack.
● Continue until everyone has had a turn.

NOW TRY THIS
1. Make more difficult codes by using more letters, or all the letters of the alphabet.
2. Write other topic words in code.

WHAT'S THE MISSING SOUND?

OBJECTIVE: to discriminate and segment all three phonemes in CVC words
LEARNING LINK: auditory
ORGANISATION: small groups
RESOURCES: sets of prepared picture cards of single items (write the initial sound and the final sound underneath each item; place a dash to show the position of the missing medial sound) for each group

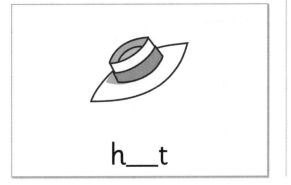

h__t

WHAT TO DO
● Place the cards face down on the table, in a pile.
● Take turns to choose a picture card.
● Look at your picture carefully. What is the picture? What is the missing sound?
● If correct, keep the card. If you are wrong, put the card at the bottom of the pile.
● The winner is the child with the most cards.

NOW TRY THIS
Shuffle the cards and then show them, one at a time, to the others. Make sure you cover the letters at the bottom! Ask the others to spell the whole word.

WHAT IS IT?

OBJECTIVE: to discriminate and spell all three phonemes in CVC words
LEARNING LINK: auditory, kinaesthetic
ORGANISATION: whole class
RESOURCES: prepare CVC words to whisper to the children; small whiteboards; dry-wipe markers, for each child

WHAT TO DO
● The teacher will whisper a three-letter word, in your ear.
● Draw a picture of the word on your whiteboard and show it to the class.
● Everyone else writes down a word for your picture, on their whiteboards.
● Now write the word for the picture on your board.
● Everyone else should check their spellings.
● Repeat the game to draw and spell more three-letter words.

NOW TRY THIS
1. Extend the game by working on spelling patterns, for example, words with consonant clusters: '*sh*ip', '*sh*op', '*sh*ed', '*sh*in'
2. You could also play this game using words with long vowel phonemes: 'sn*ake*', 'c*ake*', 'l*ake*', 'r*ake*'. Keep to one spelling pattern at a time.

WORD PUZZLE

OBJECTIVE: to discriminate and blend phonemes to read simple words

LEARNING LINK: auditory

ORGANISATION: pairs

RESOURCES: a series of picture cards placed in sets of three (arrange each set so that the initial sound from each word forms a new CVC word when blended together and, if possible, include pictures with a wide a range of initial (consonant and vowel) sounds) for each pair

CONSONANT CLUSTER WORDSEARCH

OBJECTIVE: to discriminate, read and spell words with initial consonant clusters

LEARNING LINK: tactile

ORGANISATION: individual

RESOURCES: copies of the wordsearch; felt-tipped pens or pencils, for each child

C	L	O	C	K	W
L	N	C	L	I	P
O	C	L	U	B	S
W	L	A	E	C	L
N	B	P	S	O	K

WHAT TO DO

- Look at a set of three picture cards.
- Say the first sound for each picture clearly, for example, *p-pin*; *e-egg*; *n-net*.
- Now stretch out each sound so that you say a new word: *p-e-n = pen*.
- Take turns with your partner to look at other sets of three picture cards. Work out each new word by reading the first letter sounds only.

NOW TRY THIS

1. In pairs, use sets of five picture cards to make longer words, for example, *pin – egg –net – nut – yoyo = penny*. Who can make and read the most new words?

2. In pairs, use sets of five or six picture cards to make words that have consonant clusters, for example, *cup – hen – egg – sun – ten – sun = chests*. Practise reading the new words you have made.

WHAT TO DO

- Look at the wordsearch carefully.
- Circle all the words that begin with 'cl'.
- Count the 'cl' words. How many words did you find?

NOW TRY THIS

List all of the 'cl' words that you have found. Write a sentence using each word.

ANSWERS

clock, clown, clap, clues, clip, clubs

C	L	O	C	K	W
L	N	C	L	I	P
O	C	L	U	B	S
W	L	A	E	C	L
N	B	P	S	O	K

ADD ONS

OBJECTIVE: to discriminate, read and spell words with initial consonant clusters
LEARNING LINK: auditory, tactile
ORGANISATION: pairs
RESOURCES: different coloured dry-wipe markers; small whiteboards, for each pair

WHAT TO DO

● Choose a consonant cluster that you both want to practise, for example, 'br'. Each take a different coloured marker pen.
● Write this cluster on the board (six times each).
● Use a different coloured pen to add endings to the 'br' cluster to make new words. Can you each think of six words?
● Check your spellings with the teacher or a dictionary.

NOW TRY THIS

Have a contest with your partner! Choose a different consonant cluster, for example 'gr'. See how many 'gr' words you can each write down in one minute. Use an egg-timer to remind you when a minute is up.

WHICH WORD?

OBJECTIVE: to discriminate, read and spell words with common final phonemes including consonant clusters
LEARNING LINK: auditory
ORGANISATION: individual or small groups
RESOURCES: prepare sets of word cards from photocopiable page 56, for each child or group.

WHAT TO DO

● Shuffle the cards.
● Turn the cards over, one at a time.
● Say what the picture is.
● Choose the right spelling.
● Play the game until all the picture cards have been used up.

NOW TRY THIS

1. Play the game with a partner. Shuffle the cards and fan them out. Pick a card and tell your partner what the picture is. Ask them to spell the word. Play the game until you have used all the cards.
2. Pick one of the cards and write a list of new words which end with the same consonant cluster, for example, 'dent', 'tent', 'sent', 'plant'.

DRAW AND LABEL

OBJECTIVE: to discriminate, read and spell words with common final clusters
LEARNING LINK: auditory, tactile
ORGANISATION: individual, small groups or whole class
RESOURCES: think up three silly sentences that match the end cluster being practised (see examples below); small whiteboards; dry-wipe markers, for each child

The man has a sack on his back and a red sock on his nose.

The pink drink is in a big sink.

The camel has a lamp on her hump and a stamp on her head!

WHAT TO DO

● The teacher will say a silly sentence twice. Listen carefully.
● Quickly draw on your whiteboard what you have heard.
● Label the items in your picture that have the same end cluster, for example, 'back', 'sack' 'sock'.
● Repeat for two more sentences.

NOW TRY THIS

Think of your own sentences for the others to draw. Remember to include rhyming words to label in the pictures.

SH!

OBJECTIVE: to hear and identify initial and final sounds 'sh' and 'ch'
LEARNING LINK: auditory, kinaesthetic
ORGANISATION: whole class
RESOURCES: picture cards arranged in the following order: 'shop', 'shoe', 'chin', 'ship', 'chick', 'shell', 'fish', 'church', 'dish', 'chain', 'branch', 'torch'

WHAT TO DO

● The teacher will hold up some picture cards, one at a time.
● Stand up for pictures containing the 'sh' sound and sit down for pictures containing the 'ch' sound.
● Say the sound aloud as soon as you see the picture!
● The children who are last to do the correct action are 'out'.
● The winner is the last child left in the game.

NOW TRY THIS

Play the game faster to see how many children are caught out. Remember to say the sound as soon as you see the picture.

PICTURE CLUE CROSSWORD

OBJECTIVE: to secure spelling of initial, final and medial phonemes in words
LEARNING LINK: auditory, tactile
ORGANISATION: individual or pairs
RESOURCES: copies of the picture crossword on photocopiable page 57, for each child or pair

WHAT TO DO

● Work on your own or with a partner.
● Look at the picture clues.
● Say what you see in the picture.
● Write each word into the correct spaces, on the crossword.
● Check your spellings.

NOW TRY THIS

Make up your own picture crossword for your partner to solve.

ANSWERS
Across: **1.** boat **3.** egg **5.** tap;
Down: **1.** ball **2.** tree **4.** goat

WORD FAMILY GAME

OBJECTIVE: to discriminate and read common spelling patterns containing vowel phoneme 'ea'
LEARNING LINK: auditory, tactile
ORGANISATION: individual, small groups or whole class
RESOURCES: copies of an outline of a loaf of bread with heading at top 'ea' and an outline of a bed with heading at top 'e' (see below); a list of eight words containing either the 'ea' or 'e' vowel phonemes (suggested words: 'bread', 'fled', 'thread', 'bed', 'bled', 'spread', 'tread', 'shed'); pencils, for each child

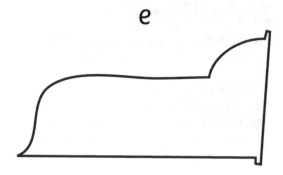

WHAT TO DO

● Read each word from your list, slowly.
● Write each word into the correct shape, depending on whether it spelled with 'ea' or 'e'.
● At the end of the session, check the work is correct.

NOW TRY THIS

1. How many more words can you think of to put in the outlines? Check your spellings with a teacher at the end.
2. Choose three words from each word family. Write sentences using the words.

LABELS

OBJECTIVE: to discriminate, read and spell the common spelling patterns for vowel phoneme 'ir'
LEARNING LINK: tactile
ORGANISATION: individual
RESOURCES: a set of picture cards showing a drawing of: a girl, a bird, a skirt, a shirt, a church; prepare cards with labels to match each picture, but muddle up the letters, for example, 'lgir'; leave writing space at bottom of each word card for the child to write the correct version

WHAT TO DO
- Look at each drawing.
- Now look at each label carefully.
- Match each label to the right picture.
- Rewrite the letters in the correct order to make a word.
- Check your spellings at the end.

NOW TRY THIS
Make up your own 'ir' word puzzle for a partner to solve. You may need to give some clues to help them to solve it.

MATCH THE SOUND

OBJECTIVE: to discriminate and read the common spelling patterns for long vowel phoneme 'air'
LEARNING LINK: auditory, tactile
ORGANISATION: whole class
RESOURCES: photocopiable page 58; pencils, for each child

WHAT TO DO
- The teacher will read the story, 'The Little Bear'.
- Follow the story and listen for all the words that have the 'air' sound.
- Circle the words with your pencil, as you hear them.
- How many 'air' words did you find?

NOW TRY THIS
Sort the 'air' words into their spelling pattern groups. How many different spelling pattern groups are there?

ASK A QUESTION

OBJECTIVE: to read words containing the digraph 'wh'
LEARNING LINK: auditory, tactile
ORGANISATION: whole class
RESOURCES: prepare some question sentences to ask the children orally, for example, 'What time is it?' (omit the question word when speaking); stick six large word cards to the board with Blu-Tack®, as follows: 'What', 'When', 'Who', 'Which', 'Why', 'Where'

WHAT TO DO
- Listen as a sentence is read out, for example, _____ is the time? (What)
- Look at the 'wh' words on the board and read aloud the card that shows the missing word.
- Play the game until all the cards have been read.

NOW TRY THIS
Shuffle the 'wh' cards and place them face down on the table. One child chooses a card. Read the card to the child. The child should spell the 'wh' word. If they spell the word correctly, they stay in the game. If incorrect, they 'sit out'.

NAME TOWERS

OBJECTIVE: to recognise critical features of words: length
LEARNING LINK: auditory
ORGANISATION: whole class
RESOURCES: a large whiteboard; red and blue board pens: choose names of children in the class and draw several blank name towers on the board, using a blue pen for a girl's name and red for a boy's name; mark the appropriate number of blocks on each tower to indicate number of letters in a child's name

WHAT TO DO
- Look at the name towers on the board.
- Take turns to guess whose name will fit within each tower.
- Do you agree with others? If not, why not?
- Repeat until all the towers on the board have been filled in with the correct child's name.

NOW TRY THIS
1. Play the game using the names of teachers, helpers, caretakers and so on.
2. Play the game at home with your family, using names of brothers, sisters, aunts or uncles … or even your neighbours

WORD TOWERS

OBJECTIVE: to recognise critical features of words: length
LEARNING LINK: auditory, kinaesthetic
ORGANISATION: pairs
RESOURCES: a large whiteboard; board pens; small whiteboards; dry-wipe markers, for each pair

WHAT TO DO

- Draw a word tower for something in the classroom.
- Draw one block on the tower for each letter in the word.
- Write one letter into the tower, in the right place.
- Ask your partner what the word is.
- Ask them to write in all the other letters.
- Check their spelling.
- Each child earns one point each time they guess their partner's word and an extra point for a correct spelling.
- The winner is the child with the most points.

NOW TRY THIS

Use this activity to practise topic words. For example, for the topic 'My body' word towers could be drawn for 'hand', 'eye', 'head', 'leg' and so on.

NAME SHAPES

OBJECTIVE: to recognise the shape of words
LEARNING LINK: tactile
ORGANISATION: small groups
RESOURCES: prepared name shapes (outlines of the children's names cut out of stiff card) for each group

WHAT TO DO

- Look at the name shapes on the table.
- Take turns to find your name shape card.
- Trace round the card with your finger, telling the others where each letter of your name would fit.

- Do the others think your choice is correct? If not, why not?
- Repeat, until all the cards have been chosen.

NOW TRY THIS

Place all the name shapes for the group or class in a bag. Pull out a name shape and try to match it to the right child. If you are right, you keep the shape. If you are wrong, you must put the name shape back in the bag. Don't call out while others are having their turn! Keep playing until all the name shapes have been matched.

WORD SHAPES

OBJECTIVE: to recognise the shape and length of words
LEARNING LINK: tactile
ORGANISATION: small groups
RESOURCES: prepared word shapes for items in the classroom (outlines cut out of stiff card, for example, 'table', 'desk', 'chair', 'window', 'door') for each group

WHAT TO DO

- Look at the word shapes on the table.
- Take turns to match each word shape card to an item in the classroom. Describe the word shape to the others, for example: *It is a long word; it has a tall letter and a hanging letter in it.*
- Do the others think you are right? If not, why not?
- Repeat, until all the word shapes have been matched.

NOW TRY THIS

Place all the word shapes in a cloth bag. Take turns to pull out a word shape and guess the word. If you are right, you may stick the shape on to the item in the classroom using Blu Tack®. If you are wrong, put the shape back into the bag. Don't call out answers during someone else's turn. Keep playing until all the word shapes have been matched.

WORD WHEEL

OBJECTIVE: to spell high frequency words
LEARNING LINK: auditory
ORGANISATION: whole class
RESOURCES: a large wheel shape drawn on the board (see below) with the following words written around the inside (no spaces) clockwise in this order: 's a i d c o m e t h e y w e n t w a s f o r m e l i k e p l a y a l l'; small whiteboards; dry-wipe markers, for each child

WHAT TO DO
● There are ten words in the wheel.
● Find the words and write them, in a list, on your whiteboard. (Clue: start with the letter 's' at the top of the board, and scan for words moving clockwise around the wheel.)

NOW TRY THIS
Can you see any smaller words within words in the wheel, for example, 'lay', 'we', 'the', 'as'?

SPOT THE RIME

OBJECTIVE: to identify rime, in words
LEARNING LINK: auditory, tactile
ORGANISATION: individual; small groups
RESOURCES: copies of the familiar nursery rhyme 'Miss Polly had a Dolly' (see below); colouring pencils, for each child

---

Miss Polly had a dolly who was sick, sick, sick.
So she phoned for the docter to come quick, quick, quick.
The doctor came with his bag and his hat,
And he knocked at the door with a rat-a-tat-tat.

He looked at the dolly and he shook his head.
He said, 'Miss Polly put her straight to bed.'
He wrote on a paper for a pill, pill, pill.
'That'll make her better, yes it will, will, will.'

WHAT TO DO
● Read the nursery rhyme.
● Circle all the words ending with 'ick', in yellow.
● Circle all the words ending with 'at', in red.
● Circle all the words ending with 'ill', in blue.
● How many 'ick' words did you find?
● How may 'at' words did you find?
● How many 'ill' words did you find?

NOW TRY THIS
Listen to the nursery rhyme again and circle words that have the 'ea' sound, as in *bread*. Remember that the 'ea' sound can also be spelled 'e', as in 'red'. Circle in pencil the words you find.

RHYMING WORD GAME

OBJECTIVE: to recognise common spelling patterns in words; to recognise words that rhyme
LEARNING LINK: auditory, tactile
ORGANISATION: pairs
RESOURCES: prepare ten word cards, in rhyming pairs, that focus on a spelling pattern, for example: 'ck' endings – 'clock', 'sock', 'flick', 'stick', 'rack', 'sack', 'neck', 'deck', 'luck', 'stuck', for each pair

WHAT TO DO
● Shuffle the cards.
● Spread the cards out face down on the table.
● Take turns to look at two cards.
● Read the words. Do they rhyme?
● If the words rhyme, keep the pair of cards.
● If they do not rhyme, return the cards to the table.
● The winner is the child with the most pairs.

NOW TRY THIS
1. Repeat the game above, but this time you must cover the cards and correctly spell the words aloud, before keeping them.
2. Place each pair of cards in rows on the table. See how many more words you can think of for each row. Write each new word on a piece of card and place in the correct row.

HIGH FREQUENCY WORDSEARCH

OBJECTIVE: to spell common irregular words
LEARNING LINK: tactile
ORGANISATION: whole class
RESOURCES: prepare the following wordsearch on a large whiteboard:

A	B	O	U	T
N	Y	R	S	I
B	A	L	L	M
M	A	Y	B	E

WHAT TO DO
● Take turns to find and highlight the 12 words hidden in the grid.
● Check each other's words.
● Keep going until you have found all 12 words.

NOW TRY THIS
Work on your own to find the words against the clock.

ANSWERS
about, an, ball, all, time, us, by, may, or, be, out, me

A	B	O	U	T
N	Y	R	S	I
B	A	L	L	M
M	A	Y	B	E

PAPER CHASE

OBJECTIVE: to spell common irregular words
LEARNING LINK: tactile
ORGANISATION: individual
RESOURCES: list five high frequency words on the board for children to find in newspapers, comics, magazines; copies of newspapers; comics; magazines; highlighter pens (five different colours) for each child

WHAT TO DO
● Look at the first words on the board. Check the order of the letters.
● Choose a highlighter pen.
● Scan your newspaper and see how many times you find that word on one page.
● Highlight the word each time you find it.

● Repeat for the other words on the board. Remember to use a different colour highlighter pen for each new word.
● Which was the most common word?

NOW TRY THIS
See how many of the words you can find on a different page of the newspaper, in one minute. Use an egg-timer to time yourself.

WORD SUMS

OBJECTIVE: to spell common irregular words
LEARNING LINK: tactile, kinaesthetic
ORGANISATION: individual
RESOURCES: sets of high frequency word cards, cut into halves, for each child

WHAT TO DO
● Shuffle the cards.
● Spread them out, face up on the table.
● Match the halves together to make whole words.
● Ask your teacher to check that they are right.

NOW TRY THIS
Turn the cards face down on the table. Turn them over, two at a time, to see if you have found the right start and ending of a word. If correct, keep the pair. If not, return the cards to the table and try again.

DRAW AND SPELL

OBJECTIVE: to use the 's' ending for plurals
LEARNING LINK: kinaesthetic
ORGANISATION: whole class
RESOURCES: a large whiteboard; board pens; draw a picture of plural items, such as 'hats', on the board

WHAT TO DO
● Look at the picture on the board
● Write the plural word to match the picture. Don't forget to add 's'.
● If you are correct, draw a new plural picture.
● A different child writes a plural word on the board, to match your picture.
● Repeat the activity to draw and spell more plural words.

NOW TRY THIS
Use this activity to explore making plurals from words ending in 'y', 'f', 'ch' or 'sh'.

SECRET MESSAGE

OBJECTIVE: to read and spell CVC and high frequency words, with increasing confidence
LEARNING LINK: auditory, tactile
ORGANISATION: whole class
RESOURCES: a secret message written on to a large whiteboard (see below); small whiteboards; dry-wipe markers, for each child

Meet me under the 🌳 by the old 🏠 at $3 + 4 + 2$ o'⏰ tonight. I will be wearing a red 🎩 and a green 🧥.

WHAT TO DO
- Read the secret message.
- Work out the words in the picture clues.
- Write out the secret message in full.
- Check your spellings.
- Ask your partner to check your message.

NOW TRY THIS
Make up your own secret message. Swap messages with your partner for them to try to solve.

DOUBLE TROUBLE

OBJECTIVE: to investigate words containing double consonants
LEARNING LINK: tactile
ORGANISATION: whole class
RESOURCES: a selection of picture cards of familiar items, whose names have medial double consonants, for example: 'kettle', 'bubble', 'fiddle', 'butter'; small whiteboards; dry-wipe markers, for each child

WHAT TO DO
- Look at the pictures, one at a time.
- Work out the double consonants in the middle of each picture's name, for example, double 't' in 'kettle'.
- Write the words on your whiteboards.
- Show your spellings to the teacher.
- Repeat until all the cards have been used up.

NOW TRY THIS
Write a sentence for each of the words you have written. At the end of the session, read your sentences aloud to the rest of the class.

FIND THE WORDS

OBJECTIVE: to find smaller words within words
LEARNING LINK: tactile
ORGANISATION: small groups
RESOURCES: write the word 'information' on the board and circle the word 'mat' within it; small whiteboards; dry-wipe markers, for each group

WHAT TO DO
- Find as many smaller words as you can in the word 'information'.
- List the words that you find.

NOW TRY THIS
Now see how many smaller words you can find in your own name.

ANSWERS
I, in, info, inform, for, or, form, format, formation, mat, at, ion

COMPOUND WORDS GAME

OBJECTIVE: to match words together to form compound words
LEARNING LINK: kinaesthetic, tactile
ORGANISATION: individual
RESOURCES: ten picture cards for words that, when joined with another card, will make a compound word, for example, sun + hat = sunhat (suggested cards: 'sun', 'flower', 'lady', 'bird', 'butter', 'fly', 'ear', 'ring', 'foot', 'ball'); five pieces of card; pencils, for each child

WHAT TO DO
- Spread the picture cards out on the table.
- Put them into pairs to make compound words.
- Write the compound words on a piece of card and place it under the pair of pictures.
- Play the game until the pairs have been matched.

NOW TRY THIS
Turn the cards face down on the table. Turn over two at a time to see if you can make a compound word. If you can, keep the pair. If you cannot, return the cards to the table and try again.

ALL CHANGE

OBJECTIVE: to discriminate onset from rime in spelling
LEARNING LINK: auditory, tactile
ORGANISATION: small groups
RESOURCES: prepared picture cards made from photocopiable page 61; pencils; paper, for each group

WHAT TO DO
- Look at the picture cards.
- Change the first consonant or cluster in each word to the new consonant.
- Say the new word
- Write the new word.

NOW TRY THIS
1. Look at one of the picture cards again. See how many new words you can make by changing the first consonant or cluster, for example, 'mouse', 'house', 'louse', 'grouse'.
2. Write a sentence using each new word you have made.
3. Have fun trying to use two or more rhyming words that you have made, in a sentence. What is the highest number of rhyming words you can use to make a good sentence?

RHYMING STRINGS

OBJECTIVE: to generate rhyming strings
LEARNING LINK: auditory, tactile
ORGANISATION: pairs
RESOURCES: small whiteboards; dry-wipe markers, for each pair

WHAT TO DO
- In pairs, think of a word to make a rhyming string, for example, 'sing'.
- One of you writes your word on the board.
- Now take turns to write a word on the list.
- Try to write as long a rhyming string of words as you can.
- Ask the teacher to check your spellings when you have finished.

NOW TRY THIS
Have a contest with a partner. Decide on a start word. See how many rhyming words you can think of in one minute. Use an egg-timer to tell you when the minute is up. Who wrote the longest string?

WRITE THE WORD

OBJECTIVE: to investigate spellings of verbs ending 'ing' (present tense verbs)
LEARNING LINK: auditory, tactile
ORGANISATION: small groups
RESOURCES: picture cards made from photocopiable page 60, for each group

WHAT TO DO
- Look at the picture cards.
- Say what the child in the picture is doing.
- Write the 'doing' word (verb) on your paper.
- Swap papers with your partner.
- Check each other's spellings.

NOW TRY THIS
Write a sentence using each of the verbs that you have found. Make sure each of your sentences starts with a capital letter and ends with a full stop.

CROCODILE ALPHABET

OBJECTIVE: to understand alphabetical order
LEARNING LINK: tactile
ORGANISATION: pairs
RESOURCES: copies of the crocodile alphabet (enlarged to A3) on photocopiable page 59, for each child; colouring pencils, for each pair

WHAT TO DO
- Look at the letters on the crocodile's back.
- Track the alphabet in the right order, colouring in the circles each time.
- Swap crocodiles with your partner.
- Check each other's work.

NOW TRY THIS
Take new copies of the crocodile alphabet and try tracking the alphabet backwards!

TAKE AWAYS

OBJECTIVE: to recognise smaller words within words
LEARNING LINK: kinaesthetic, tactile
ORGANISATION: pairs
RESOURCES: prepare subtraction word cards (see below); small whiteboards; dry-wipe markers, for each pair

window – ow =	
card – d =	
farm – f =	
caterpillar – cater =	
robin – ro =	

WHAT TO DO

● Look at the cards.
● Say the word. Write the word.
● Take away (rub out) the letters shown in the subtraction word sum.
● Read the new word that you have made.

NOW TRY THIS

Write the new words you have made into sentences. Make sure each of your sentences starts with a capital letter and ends with a full stop.

CHOP, CHOP!

OBJECTIVE: to note syllable boundaries in words
LEARNING LINK: auditory, kinaesthetic, tactile
ORGANISATION: whole class
RESOURCES: slips of paper; scissors; pencils, for each child

WHAT TO DO

● Write your first name on the slip of paper.
● Say your name aloud a few times.
● How many syllable beats are in your name? (Clapping or nodding to the syllable beats may help.)
● Draw lines through your name to mark where each syllable ends. Cut your name up into syllables.
● Show the syllables in your name to your partner, or to the rest of the class.

NOW TRY THIS

Repeat the activity, to find the syllables in your last name.

SPELLING THE DAYS OF THE WEEK

OBJECTIVE: to spell days of the week
LEARNING LINK: tactile, visual
ORGANISATION: small groups of seven
RESOURCES: days of the week word cards, for each group

WHAT TO DO

● Place the word cards in the right order.
● Take turns to choose a card and hide it, so that no one can see the spelling.
● Choose a child to spell the day on your card.
● If correct, that child gets a point.
● Play the game until all the children have spelled at least one day.
● Add up the points to find the winner.

NOW TRY THIS

1. At the start of the activity make sure your group know that Monday is to be day number one. Each child, in turn, calls out a number from 1–7, and the name of another child in the group. The child chosen has to work out which day matches the number and then spells out the day.
2. Make this game harder by spelling the number as well as the day.

SOUNDS AND LETTERS

OBJECTIVE: to say the letters of the alphabet in order
LEARNING LINK: kinaesthetic
ORGANISATION: small groups or whole class, standing in a circle
RESOURCES: use a large copy of the alphabet to check that children know the order of the letters

WHAT TO DO

● One child starts the alphabet round. They say the letter and then the sound it makes, for example, for 'A' say *a*.
● Continue around the circle, until the alphabet is complete.

NOW TRY THIS

Repeat the activity saying the alphabet backwards!

THE ALPHABET SONG

OBJECTIVE: to understand alphabetical order, in songs
LEARNING LINK: visual
ORGANISATION: whole class
RESOURCES: use a large copy of the alphabet to check that children can say the letters of the alphabet in order, before the activity

WHAT TO DO

● Sing the traditional alphabet song from the board:

> A B C D E F G,
>
> H I J K L M N O P,
>
> Q R S T U V,
>
> W X Y and Z.
>
> Now I know my ABC
>
> You can sing along with me.

● Now sing the song from memory.

NOW TRY THIS

The teacher claps for each letter of the alphabet. When the teacher stops clapping, you must shout out what the next letter is.

SPOT THE RHYME

OBJECTIVE: to recognise, explore and work with rhyming patterns
LEARNING LINK: visual
ORGANISATION: small groups
RESOURCES: five lists of rhyming words, with one non-rhyming word per list (see below) for each group

WHAT TO DO

● One member of your group reads out the lists of words, one list at a time.
● Listen for the word that doesn't rhyme each time.
● One child gives the answer and writes the word on the board.
● One point is scored for every correct answer.
● The winner is the child with the most points.

NOW TRY THIS

1. Make up your own lists of rhyming words. Include one word that doesn't rhyme. See if your group can spot the odd word out, in your list.
2. Play the game again but this time make it even harder by including two words that don't rhyme and three words that do. How quickly can your group find the two odd words?

> 1) bed, red, led, lad, fed
>
> 2) pit, met, sit, lit, kit
>
> 3) rang, sang, sung, bang, fang
>
> 4) luck, buck, suck, tack, duck
>
> 5) will, fill, sill, bill, bell

NURSERY RHYME TIME

OBJECTIVE: to recognise, explore and work with rhyming patterns
LEARNING LINK: tactile, visual
ORGANISATION: individual or small groups
RESOURCES: colouring pencils; copies of traditional nursery rhymes such as 'Humpty Dumpty', for each child

WHAT TO DO
- Read or sing the nursery rhyme.
- How many different rhyming patterns can you find?
- Circle the words that have the same rhyming patterns. Use a different colouring pencil for each new rhyming pattern.

NOW TRY THIS
Write the words that have the same rhyming patterns in lists on your whiteboard. See if you can add new rhyming words to each list.

FIND THE RHYME

OBJECTIVE: to recognise, explore and work with rhyming patterns
LEARNING LINK: visual
ORGANISATION: pairs
RESOURCES: compose short poems, on card, which have missing words on alternate rhyming lines (see suggestion below); small whiteboards; dry-wipe markers, for each pair

> Jack had a cat
> But the cat was _____
>
> It slept all day.
> It wouldn't _____
>
> It wouldn't run.
> So it wasn't any _____!

WHAT TO DO
- One person reads the poem, two lines at a time.
- Your partner thinks of a word to rhyme at the end of each second line.
- Your partner writes the word on the whiteboard.
- At the end of the poem, check that the words written by your partner fit the rhyme.
- Check all spellings carefully.

NOW TRY THIS
Together, make up a short poem. See if other children in your class can guess and spell the missing words.

ANSWERS
fat, play, fun

THE WHEELS ON THE BUS

OBJECTIVE: to explore repeating patterns in songs and rhymes
LEARNING LINK: kinaesthetic
ORGANISATION: whole class
RESOURCES: a copy of the children's song: 'The Wheels on the Bus'

WHAT TO DO
- Sing the song 'The Wheels on the Bus.'
- Listen carefully for all the repeating words, for example, *round and round; swish, swish, swish; chatter, chatter, chatter.*
- As a class, choose some actions for each repeating set of words.
- Sing the song again, listening for the repeating patterns. Do the correct action for the words.
- Sing the song again. What was the start sound in each set of repeating words?

NOW TRY THIS
Repeat the activity for a different song, such as, 'Miss Polly had a Dolly' (see page 13).

WHO AM I?

OBJECTIVE: to hear and identify initial phonemes in names
LEARNING LINK: visual
ORGANISATION: whole class
RESOURCES: none

WHAT TO DO
- On your turn, give two clues about another child in the class, plus the first sound of the child's name.
- The rest of the class guesses who it is.
- If someone guesses correctly they will take a turn to give clues and the initial sound of another child's name.

NOW TRY THIS
Give clues for the names of teachers, teaching assistants, helpers or the caretaker.

I SPY IN THE CLASSROOM

OBJECTIVE: to hear and identify initial phonemes in words

LEARNING LINK: visual

ORGANISATION: whole class or small groups

RESOURCES: use flash cards to check that children can identify initial letter sounds, before playing the game

WHAT TO DO

- For this game you can only use items in the classroom.
- When it is your turn, say: *I spy with my little eye, something beginning with…*.Then say the start sound of the item you are thinking of. Say the letter sound, not the letter name.
- Remember, don't call out. Put up your hand if you think you know the answer.
- The child who guesses correctly chooses the next item.

NOW TRY THIS

Play again, giving the last sound of the item you are thinking of. Change the rhyme to: *I spy with my little eye, something ending with…*.

I SPY IN THE PLAYGROUND

OBJECTIVE: to hear and identify initial phonemes in words

LEARNING LINK: kinaesthetic, tactile

ORGANISATION: whole class

RESOURCES: a playground or hall; use flash cards of initial letters, to check that children can identify sounds, before the game

WHAT TO DO

- For this game you can only use objects in the playground.
- When it is your turn, say: *I Spy with my little eye, something beginning with…*.Then say the first letter of the item you are thinking of.
- Remember not to call out. Put up your hand if you think you know the answer.
- If chosen to guess, run and touch the item you think begins with that letter.
- The child who guesses correctly chooses the next item.

NOW TRY THIS

Play again, giving the last letter of the item you are thinking of. Change the rhyme to: *I Spy with my little eye, something ending with…*.

FIVES

OBJECTIVE: to hear and identify initial phonemes in words

LEARNING LINK: tactile

ORGANISATION: small groups

RESOURCES: a cloth bag and letter tiles, for each group

WHAT TO DO

- Place the letter tiles in the cloth bag.
- Shake the bag well.
- One child takes out a tile and says the letter sound.
- The child then chooses another member of the group to say five words that begin with that letter sound.
- If their five words are correct, hand this child the bag to take out the next letter tile.
- Play the game until all the letters have been used up.

NOW TRY THIS

See if you can think of ten words that begin with each letter.

CHOOSE A LETTER

OBJECTIVE: to hear and identify initial phonemes in words

LEARNING LINK: –

ORGANISATION: small groups; whole class

RESOURCES: none

WHAT TO DO

- Stand in a circle.
- One child chooses a letter.
- In turn, say a word beginning with that letter, until the teacher says *change!*
- On the word *change*, the next child has to think of a new letter and say a word that begins with it.
- Continue to say words beginning with the new letter, until the teacher says *change* again.
- If a child cannot think of a word, they sit down and are 'out'.
- The winner is the last child standing.

NOW TRY THIS

1. Try and think of two words for each sound. You cannot repeat a word, so you must think very hard!

2. Repeat the game but this time think of words that end with the chosen letter.

WIGGLY WOO!

OBJECTIVE: to hear and identify initial phonemes in words
LEARNING LINK: kinaesthetic
ORGANISATION: whole class
RESOURCES: a hall or playground; words for the song 'Wiggly Woo' (see below)

There's a worm at the bottom of the garden,

And his name is Wiggly Woo.

There's a worm at the bottom of the garden,

And all that he can do,

Is wiggle all night

And wiggle all day.

Whatever else the people do say,

There's a worm at the bottom of the garden,

And his name is Wiggly Woo.

(repeat)

WHAT TO DO
● Practise the words of the song.
● Listen while the song is sung and then wiggle when you hear a word beginning with 'w'.
● Sing the song together.

NOW TRY THIS
Listen to the song again. Wiggle when you hear rhyming words 'woo/ do'; 'day/ say'.

SING AND SPELL

OBJECTIVE: to recognise the critical features of words: common spelling patterns
LEARNING LINK: –
ORGANISATION: whole class
RESOURCES: words for the popular song: 'I'm H-A-P-P-Y' (see below); a list of other words ending in 'y'

I'm H-A-P-P-Y,
I'm H-A-P-P-Y,
I know I am,
I'm sure I am,
I'm H-A-P-P-Y!

WHAT TO DO
● Sing the song 'I'm H-A-P-P-Y!', remembering to spell out the word 'Happy'.
● Now repeat the song, changing the word 'happy' for other 'y'-ending words such as 'merry', 'jolly' and so on.
● Listen carefully to the spelling pattern as you spell out the 'y'-ending word.

NOW TRY THIS
Think of other 'y'-ending words that they could sing and spell – the funnier the better, for example, 'silly', 'soggy', 'messy'.

WHAT AM I?

OBJECTIVE: to hear and identify initial phonemes in words
LEARNING LINK: visual
ORGANISATION: whole class
RESOURCES: prepare a set of five riddle cards to read aloud to the class (see suggestions below)

I am hot. I shine during the day. I begin with **s**. What am I?

You put me on your head. I can be woolly. I begin with **h**. What am I?

You put me on your feet. I keep your feet warm. I begin with **s**. What am I?

You make me from bread. I am hot and crunchy. I begin with **t**. What am I?

You can throw me. You can bounce me too. I begin with **b**. What am I?

WHAT TO DO
● The teacher will read a riddle to you.
● Put up your hand if you know the answer.
● Guess the answer and spell the word.
● When the riddle has been solved, listen to the next one.
● Play until all the riddles have been solved.

NOW TRY THIS
Think of some more riddles to try out on your group. Who solved the most riddles?

ANSWERS
1. sun   **2.** hat   **3.** sock   **3.** toast   **4.** ball

I WENT TO MARKET

OBJECTIVE: to hear and identify initial phonemes in words
LEARNING LINK: –
ORGANISATION: small groups
RESOURCES: none

WHAT TO DO

- Sit in a circle.
- Choose someone to start the game.
- Think of a start letter, for example, 'b'.
- Everyone thinks of items that begin with this letter.
- One child starts the game by saying, for example: *I went to market and I bought a bat.*
- The next child adds to the shopping list, for example: *I went to market and I bought a bat and a ball.*
- Continue round the circle with each child adding an item that has the same start sound to the list. An item cannot be bought more than once.

NOW TRY THIS

Make the game harder by thinking of things with the same first consonant cluster, such as, 'st'– 'stick', 'stop', 'story'.

SOUND IN THE MIDDLE

OBJECTIVE: to secure identification and reading of initial, final and medial letter sounds in CVC words
LEARNING LINK: tactile, visual
ORGANISATION: small groups
RESOURCES: ten flash cards showing three CVC words in which only the medial vowel varies (see suggestions below) for each group

cat, cot, cut	bet, but, bit
tip, tap, top	hot, hit, hat
pin, pan, pen	fan, fin, fun
get, got, gut	bag, beg, big
nut, nit, net	did, dad, dud

WHAT TO DO

- Choose a caller and place all the cards face down on the table.
- The caller takes a card and reads the three words aloud.
- Listen to each word carefully and write each one down. Sound the words out loud if it helps you.
- Check your spellings with the others in the group.
- How many children spelled all the words correctly?

NOW TRY THIS

Place the cards face down on the table. Take turns to look at each card and read the three words. Keep the card if you read all three words correctly. The winner is the child with the most cards.

COLOUR FUN GAME

OBJECTIVE: to hear and identify initial phonemes in words
LEARNING LINK: –
ORGANISATION: whole class
RESOURCES: none

WHAT TO DO

- The teacher gives a sound to one child, who starts the game.
- The first child must say a colour and an item that both begin with the same letter – the funnier the pair the better, for example: *pink potatoes* or *green goats.*
- Continue round the circle until everyone has had a turn.
- Change the first letter sound when you wish.

NOW TRY THIS

Sit in a circle and play the game as quickly as possible. See how long it takes to get back to the start!

CAT AND DOG GAME

OBJECTIVE: to hear and identifying initial sounds in words
LEARNING LINK: kinaesthetic
ORGANISATION: whole class (teacher/adult-led)
RESOURCES: suggested word list: 'cat', 'dog', 'dinosaur', 'daisy', 'cube', 'cabbage', 'drawing', 'carrots', 'class', 'dinner', 'double', 'car', 'drum', 'cricket', 'duck', 'cake', 'cone', 'den', 'desert', 'crab'

WHAT TO DO
● Sit on the carpet and listen carefully to a list of words.
● If a word begins with 'd', then say *woof, woof*! If a word begins with 'c', then say *miaow*!
● If a child makes the wrong animal sound they are 'out'.
● The winner(s) are those who are still in the game by the end of the list.

NOW TRY THIS
1. Write a new word list of words with 'f' or 'h' first letter sounds and play the game again. If children hear words beginning with 'f', they say *croak, croak*! If children hear words beginning with 'h', they say *cluck, cluck*!
2. The adult will make this game harder by reading aloud a new list of words with 'p', 't' or 'h' as first letter sounds. If a word begins with 'p' then pat your head. If a word begins with 't' tap your feet. If a word begins with 'h' then hum.

CHINESE WHISPERS

OBJECTIVE: to secure identification and spelling of initial, final and medial sounds in words
LEARNING LINK: –
ORGANISATION: small groups
RESOURCES: none

WHAT TO DO
● The teacher thinks of a word.
● The teacher whispers this word to the child next to them.
● The whisper is passed around the circle.
● The last child in the group has to say the word and spell it correctly.
● If correct, the teacher whispers a new word for the child to pass on.

NOW TRY THIS
Try passing on two words each time.

FIVE QUESTIONS GAME

OBJECTIVE: to secure identification, spelling and reading of initial, final and medial sounds in words
LEARNING LINK: –
ORGANISATION: whole class
RESOURCES: none

WHAT TO DO
● The teacher thinks of a word (such as 'plum') and tells the class what the topic (such as 'fruits') is.
● Ask five questions to help you guess the word. The teacher will only answer *yes* or *no*.
● After five questions, one child should guess the word and spell it.
● If correct, the child thinks of a new topic word for the others to guess and spell.

NOW TRY THIS
Play the game again, but this time the answer can be guessed before the five questions have been asked. Who can guess correctly with the fewest number of clues?

SPELLING LINE

OBJECTIVE: to secure identification, spelling and reading of initial, final and medial sounds in words
LEARNING LINK: –
ORGANISATION: whole class, divided into four teams, standing in lines
RESOURCES: words associated with current class projects

WHAT TO DO
● In turn, the teacher gives each team a word to spell.
● Spell the word as a team, saying one letter each, in the correct sequence.
● If correct, the team wins a point.
● The winning team is the one with the most points.

NOW TRY THIS
Spell the word forwards and backwards to earn an extra point!

NAIRB

AUDITORY LEARNING

SPELL AND SHOW

OBJECTIVE: to secure phonemic spelling
LEARNING LINK: visual, tactile
ORGANISATION: whole class
RESOURCES: prepare a list of ten words, for example, words focusing on a specific spelling pattern; small whiteboards; dry-wipe markers, for each child

WHAT TO DO
● The teacher will read a list of ten words. Each word will be said twice.
● Split each word into the sounds that you can hear.
● Write the words on your boards.
● Now swap whiteboards with your partner and check their spellings.
● Correct any mistakes.

NOW TRY THIS
Repeat the activity, but this time, write each word within a sentence (remember to write in full sentences on your board). Swap boards with your partner and check their spellings. Correct any mistakes.

THE LISTENING GAME

OBJECTIVE: to discriminate and segment phonemes in words
LEARNING LINK: visual
ORGANISATION: small groups
RESOURCES: five lists of words, suggestions are as follows: 1. (t) ant/ ate/ tan; 2. (p) map/ pot/ ape; 3. (s): bus/ sip/ ask; 4. (g): got/ bag/ age; 5. (l): lit/ will/ pile (you may need to revise split digraphs a-e; i-e, before the activity) for each group

WHAT TO DO
● Choose a child to read out each list of words, for example, ant, ate, tan.
● Listen for the same sound in each list, for example, 't'.
● Ask the others to tell you where the 't' sound appears in each word; either start, middle or end.
● Play the game until all the lists have been read out.

NOW TRY THIS
Each member of the group writes a list of words with the sound 'n' appearing in different places in each word, for example, 'nut', 'hen', 'cone'. Take turns to read your lists aloud. Can the others spot where the 'n' is hiding?

TONGUE TWISTERS

OBJECTIVE: to discriminate and identify words with initial consonant clusters
LEARNING LINK: visual
ORGANISATION: small groups
RESOURCES: prepare sets of five tongue twisters (see suggestions below) written on pieces of card, for each group

Brown bears break lots of broad branches.

Clever Claude climbs trees but clings on tightly.

Creepy crawlies creep about in cracks in the rocks.

Tracy tripped treading over toy train tracks.

Strands of string can be very strong.

WHAT TO DO
● One child reads the first tongue twister aloud.
● The rest of the group must listen out for 'br' sounds.
● Count how many words begin with that sound.
● Go over the tongue twister again to check that the answers are correct.
● Continue until all the tongue twisters have been read out.

NOW TRY THIS
Make up your own tongue twisters for different consonant clusters. Read them out to the others. Ask them to find and count the clusters you have used.

CIRCLE ALPHABET

OBJECTIVE: to understand alphabetical order
LEARNING LINK: kinaesthetic
ORGANISATION: whole class, sitting in a circle
RESOURCES: use a large copy of the alphabet to check that children can say the phonetic alphabet, before the activity

WHAT TO DO
● One child starts the alphabet letter sound game.
● The child will say the first letter sound and name something that begins with that letter, for example, *a is for apple*.
● Take turns around the circle. Each child says the next letter sound and gives a word that begins with that sound.

NOW TRY THIS
Try saying the letter sounds of the alphabet backwards. Remember to say a word that begins with each of the letter sounds.

WORD CHAINS

OBJECTIVE: to discriminate and identify words with initial consonant clusters
LEARNING LINK: –
ORGANISATION: small groups (teacher/adult-led)
RESOURCES: none

WHAT TO DO
● The teacher thinks of a consonant cluster, for example 'pl'.
● In turn, go round the group with everyone thinking of a word that starts with that cluster, for example, *plant, plain, plot, plate* and so on.
● How long a word chain can your group make?

NOW TRY THIS
Choose more consonant clusters and see which of them gives you the longest word chain.

LISTEN TO THE STORY

OBJECTIVE: to identify long vowel phonemes in speech and writing
LEARNING LINK: visual
ORGANISATION: small groups
RESOURCES: a story containing a recurring long vowel phoneme (see suggestion below) for each group

> Goat wanted a ride in his boat.
> He put on a coat.
> 'This coat will keep me warm,' he gloated.
> Goat got in the boat.
> But the boat didn't float.
> The boat sank. Goat got soaked!

WHAT TO DO
● Listen to the story.
● As you listen, try to spot words that have the 'oa' sound in them – including all repeated words.
● Count these words.
● How many children counted the right number of words?

NOW TRY THIS
Make up your own short stories, focusing on a long vowel phoneme. Read this to the rest of the group while they spot the long vowel phoneme words.

ANSWER
12

MAGIC 'E' GAME

OBJECTIVE: to learn the common spelling patterns for long vowel phonemes

LEARNING LINK: visual

ORGANISATION: small groups (teacher/ adult-led)

RESOURCES: a list of ten CVC words, as follows: 'cap', 'tub', 'bit', 'hop', 'rat', 'pin', 'us', 'pan', 'hat', 'cub', for each group

WHAT TO DO

● The teacher reads the list of three-letter words, one at a time.

● Take turns to add an 'e' to the end of each word.

● Say the new word aloud and listen carefully. How has the vowel sound changed?

● Practise spelling the new word without looking at it.

● Repeat until all the words end in an 'e'.

NOW TRY THIS

As a group, think of more three-letter words and make them into new words by adding 'e' to the end. Write your new words on paper.

WHAT'S MISSING?

OBJECTIVE: to identify long vowel phonemes in speech and writing

LEARNING LINK: –

ORGANISATION: whole class

RESOURCES: prepare sentence cards that provide clues for five words (see suggestions below); write on the board the corresponding answer words, with target letters missing, for example 'tr_ _ n', 'm_ _ n', 'b_ _ t', 'sh_ _ p', 'r_ _ n'

I run on tracks. I start with **tr** and end with **n**. What's missing?
Spell me. _____

I shine at night. I start with **m** and end with **n**. What's missing?
Spell me. _____

I sail on the sea. I start with **b** and end with **t**. What's missing?
Spell me. _____

I say 'baa'. I start with **sh** and end with **p**. What's missing?
Spell me. _____

I am water from the sky. I start with **r** and end with **n**. What's missing?
Spell me. _____

WHAT TO DO

● The teacher will read a set of clues for a word.

● Use the clues to work out the missing middle sound.

● Tell the teacher the missing middle sound and then spell and say the whole word.

● Who got the most words right?

NOW TRY THIS

Now make up more questions for your partner like the ones above. Award one mark for every correct answer.

> **ANSWERS**
> **1.** train, **2.** moon, **3.** boat, **4.** sheep, **5.** rain

LONG AND SHORT

OBJECTIVE: to identify phonemes in speech and writing

LEARNING LINK: –

ORGANISATION: small groups; whole class

RESOURCES: a list of ten words containing short and long vowel phonemes, as follows: 'wet', 'wheel', 'boat', 'get', 'mean', 'men', 'flick', 'float', 'den', 'bean', for each group

WHAT TO DO

● The teacher reads out ten words, pausing after each word.

● Listen to the middle sound in each word. Is it long or short?

● Say *long* for long vowel sounds and *short* for short sounds.

● Continue until all the words in the list have been read out.

NOW TRY THIS

Think of other words with long or short middle vowel sounds. Spell the words out loud and ask the others to check if you are right.

LETTER BINGO

OBJECTIVE: to read letters that represent a–z and diagraphs 'ch', 'sh', 'th'

LEARNING LINK: visual

ORGANISATION: small groups of six

RESOURCES: five bingo cards, each with a total of nine different letters and digraphs (each bingo card must include at least two of these digraphs: sh, ch, th); a cloth bag containing letters a–z and diagraphs ch, sh, th; counters, for each group

b	ch	p
sh	r	x
a	m	th

WHAT TO DO

● Each member of the group has a bingo card.
● Place a pile of counters in the middle of the table so that all the players can reach them.
● One child acts as caller and shakes the bag of letters.
● The caller takes out letters, one at a time, and says the letter sound (without showing the letter to the group).
● If you have the sound on your bingo card, place a counter over it.
● The winner is the first player to cover all the squares on their bingo card.

NOW TRY THIS

Now play the game again, but this time, the caller says the letter name and not the sound.

SPELLING BINGO

OBJECTIVE: to investigate and spell words with 'ed' (past tense), 'ing' (present tense) endings

LEARNING LINK: tactile, visual

ORGANISATION: groups of four

RESOURCES: three bingo cards, as listed below, each with four words written on them; a set of word cards as follows: 'hop', 'sing', 'jump', 'walk', 'win', 'help', 'run', 'talk', 'swim', 'fly', 'wash', 'want'; counters; a cloth bag, for each group

hopping	singing
jumped	walked

winning	helped
running	talked

swimming	flying
washed	wanted

WHAT TO DO

● Choose a caller for your group and hand out the bingo cards and counters.
● Put the word cards in the bag and shake the bag well.
● The caller will show you a word card, one at a time, and will say each word out loud.
● Now look at your bingo card. If the word being shown matches the first part of a word on your card, cover it over with a counter.
● The winner is the first player to cover all their words and shout *bingo*.

NOW TRY THIS

Play a different game. This time the caller must pick letters out of the bag, as fast as they can. The letters in the bag spell the words on the bingo cards. The winner is the first to cover all their letters and read aloud their words.

CHILDREN'S NAMES

OBJECTIVE: to discriminate orally the number of syllables in multi-syllabic words: children's names

LEARNING LINK: kinaesthetic

ORGANISATION: whole class

RESOURCES: none

WHAT TO DO

● Sit in a circle.
● The first child says their name and how many syllable beats it has.
● They clap out the syllable beats.
● Everyone copies, by saying the name and clapping out the syllables.
● Continue until everyone's name has been clapped out in syllables.

NOW TRY THIS

Extend this game by asking children to clap out the syllables in their full names, including surnames.

WHICH ANIMAL?

OBJECTIVE: to spell common words: animal names
LEARNING LINK: –
ORGANISATION: small groups or whole class
RESOURCES: a cloth bag; animal name cards, such as: 'sheep', 'dog', 'cat' 'duck' 'bird'

WHAT TO DO

- Choose a person to be the first caller
- The caller takes a card out of the bag and reads it silently.
- Next, the caller makes the animal's noise.
- The teacher will choose someone to guess the animal and to spell its name, aloud.
- If correct, that child is the caller and takes the next card from the bag.
- Continue until the bag is empty.

NOW TRY THIS

Make the game harder by giving a brief description of the animal instead of making the animal noise.

COUNT THE SYLLABLES

OBJECTIVE: to discriminate orally the number of syllables in multi-syllabic words, using words from their reading
LEARNING LINK: –
ORGANISATION: small groups
RESOURCES: a selection of words collected during guided reading (include words of one, two, three and four syllables, for example, car (1), flower (2), butterfly (3), television (4)) for each group

WHAT TO DO

- The teacher says a word from your reading.
- Guess how many syllables that word has.
- Do the others agree?
- If necessary, clap out the syllables to check the number.
- Continue until you have practised words with up to four syllables.

NOW TRY THIS

1. Look through your reading books. Try to find as long a word as possible. Who can find the longest word? How many syllables does it have?
2. Think of all the teachers' names in the school. Who has the most syllables in their name? Who has the fewest? Remember to include syllable beats in their titles, for example, 'Miss Robinson' or 'Mr Smith'.

SYLLABLE SING-SONG

OBJECTIVE: to discriminate orally the number of syllables in multi-syllabic words, using words from their reading
LEARNING LINK: visual
ORGANISATION: small groups
RESOURCES: copies of traditional nursery rhymes, such as, 'Twinkle, Twinkle Little Star'

WHAT TO DO

- In your group sing through the nursery rhyme 'Twinkle, Twinkle Little Star'.
- Now sing it again, but this time, count all the words of two syllables.
- How many words of two syllables are there?
- List these words.

NOW TRY THIS

1. Count how many words have one or three syllables.
2. Repeat the activity using other nursery rhymes.

> **ANSWER**
> There are 10 words with two syllables.

MUSICAL NAMES!

OBJECTIVE: to discriminate orally the number of syllables in multi-syllabic words: children's names
LEARNING LINK: tactile
ORGANISATION: small groups or whole class
RESOURCES: chime bars; beaters

WHAT TO DO

- Sit in a circle.
- One child has a set of chime bars.
- They think of a child's name in the group or class and tap out the syllables of that person's name on the chime bars.
- The rest of the group guesses whose name has been tapped out.
- The child who guesses correctly has a turn on the chime bars.

NOW TRY THIS

Try tapping out the syllables in the names of teachers and helpers in school for other children in your group to guess. Remember to include the syllable beats in their titles (Miss/Mr) as well as for the name.

MUSICAL PUZZLE

OBJECTIVE: to discriminate orally the number of syllables in multi-syllabic words: children's names
LEARNING LINK: tactile
ORGANISATION: small groups or whole class
RESOURCES: a drum

WHAT TO DO
- Sit in a circle.
- One child has a drum.
- They think of a word from a class a topic, for example 'animals', and tap out the syllables of that word using the drum.
- The rest of the group guesses the word that has been tapped out.
- The person who guesses correctly has a turn on the drum.

NOW TRY THIS
Once you have guessed the animal, try to spell the whole word.

COLOUR SPELLING

OBJECTIVE: to secure reading and spelling of common words: colour names
LEARNING LINK: –
ORGANISATION: small groups (teacher/adult-led)
RESOURCES: prepare clues for colour names, for each group, for example, 'I am the colour of the sky. Spell me.'

WHAT TO DO
- The teacher gives a short clue about the colour that they want you to spell.
- The first child to spell the colour correctly gets a point.
- Continue until the group has spelled the most common colour words.
- The winner is the child with the most points.

NOW TRY THIS
Extend this activity to include more difficult or unusual colour words, such as purple, grey, orange, crimson, violet and so on.

SOUNDS THE SAME!

OBJECTIVE: to investigate and classify words with the same sounds but different spellings: homophones
LEARNING LINK: visual
ORGANISATION: small groups (teacher/adult-led)
RESOURCES: a table-top whiteboard; dry-wipe markers; ten pairs of homophones, as follows: see/sea; hare/ hair; bow/bough; night/knight; fare/fair; great/grate; thrown/ throne; tail/ tale; beech/beach; fur/fir, for each group

WHAT TO DO
- The teacher reads two words that sound the same but are spelled differently.
- When asked, give two possible spellings and write them on the board.
- If the spellings are correct, explain the meanings of the words.
- Repeat for different words.

NOW TRY THIS
In your group, try to think of other words that sound the same but are spelled differently. How many words can you think of? Write the words on the board.

SINGLE OR DOUBLE?

OBJECTIVE: to investigate and learn spellings of verbs with the 'ing' (present tense) ending
LEARNING LINK: –
ORGANISATION: whole class
RESOURCES: a list of ten 'ing' ending verbs, some having a double consonant before the 'ing' ending and some without, for example: 'jumping', 'running', 'hopping', 'singing', 'swimming', 'walking', 'hoping', 'eating', 'shopping', 'talking'

WHAT TO DO
- Listen as the teacher reads out a list of verbs. Remember, some verbs have a double consonant before adding 'ing' and others do not.
- After each verb is read, say *double* for verbs with a double consonant before the 'ing' and *single* if there is only one consonant.
- Continue until all the words on the list have been read out.

NOW TRY THIS
Try to spell out loud the words on the list. Check your spelling with the teacher or the rest of the class.

EASY ANIMAL RIDDLES

OBJECTIVE: to build collections of new words linked to topics: animals
LEARNING LINK: auditory, visual
ORGANISATION: small groups
RESOURCES: a series of short animal riddles written on to card (see examples below); write answers on the reverse of each card and make card sets; small whiteboards; dry-wipe markers, for each group

---

I wag my tail. I bark. What am I?

I lay eggs. I cluck. What am I?

I like mice. I purr. What am I?

I moo. I give milk. What am I?

I am little. I squeak. What am I?

WHAT TO DO

● Take turns to choose a riddle card and read it aloud. Don't look at the back of the card!
● Guess the name of the animal.
● Write this name on your board.
● Turn over the card to see if you are right.
● Carry on playing until all the cards have been used up.

NOW TRY THIS

1. Think of more animal riddles for the others to solve.
2. Choose a riddle card and read it. Don't read the card out loud. Make the animal noise for the others to guess.

ANSWERS
1. dog **2.** hen **3.** cat **4.** cow **5.** mouse

SPEED SPELL

OBJECTIVE: to secure reading and spelling of high frequency words
LEARNING LINK: –
ORGANISATION: pairs
RESOURCES: a list of around 50 high frequency words; a stopwatch, for each pair

WHAT TO DO

● Set your stopwatch for two minutes.
● Read a word from the list to your partner.
● Ask your partner to spell it aloud.
● If correct, award one point.
● Continue until the time is up.
● Record the number of correct spellings.
● Swap roles, by asking your partner to read some words to you.
● Record the number of correct spellings.
● Who got the higher number of correct spellings?

NOW TRY THIS

Set your stopwatch to one minute. Now see how many words your partner can spell correctly in the time.

ABACUS SPELLING GAME

OBJECTIVE: to spell longer words with increasing confidence
LEARNING LINK: visual
ORGANISATION: pairs
RESOURCES: two lists of words (containing words from two to eight letters, examples as follows:
List 1: 'in', 'hop', 'heat', 'sheet', 'window', 'animals', 'elephant'; List 2: 'at', 'run', 'snow', 'sleet', 'shadow', 'dinners', 'football') for each pair

WHAT TO DO

● Read the words from your list to your partner.
● Ask your partner to spell each word.
● If they spell a word correctly, read the next word for them to spell.
● Stop when they spell a word incorrectly.
● What was the longest word spelled?
● Now swap and ask your partner to test your spelling using their list.
● Which is the longest word you can spell?

NOW TRY THIS

Make up your own spelling lists in the same way. Test each other to see who can spell the longest word.

TEN GREEN BOTTLES

OBJECTIVE: to spell numbers to 20
LEARNING LINK: –
ORGANISATION: small groups
RESOURCES: words for the song 'Ten Green Bottles', for each group

WHAT TO DO

● Sing 'Ten Green Bottles'.
● At then end of the last line of each verse, pause while everyone calls out the spelling for the number word, for example, *n-i-n-e – nine*!
● Then carry on singing the song until all the bottles have fallen off the wall.

NOW TRY THIS

Change the song so that you spell the number words to twenty. Start with 20 Green Bottles.

SING THE WEEK

OBJECTIVE: to spell days of the week
LEARNING LINK: –
ORGANISATION: whole class
RESOURCES: teach the children the words for 'The week' song as follows:

> It's Monday today.
> It's Monday today.
> It's M-O-N-D-A-Y,
> It's Monday today.

WHAT TO DO

● To the tune 'Happy Birthday to you', sing 'The week' song.
● On the third line spell, the day.
● Repeat the song until you have sung and spelled all the days of the week.

NOW TRY THIS

Sing the song at a faster speed and try not to get in a muddle with the spellings!

SCHOOL NAME SONG

OBJECTIVE: to spell the school name
LEARNING LINK: –
ORGANISATION: whole class
RESOURCES: song words as below: change the name of the school on the last line, as appropriate

> This is the way we spell our school,
> Spell our school, spell our school.
> This is the way we spell our school,
> On a cold and frosty morning.
> T-O-D-S-T-O-N...Todston!

WHAT TO DO

● To the tune of 'Here we go Round the Mulberry Bush', sing the song and spell the name of your school.

NOW TRY THIS

Change the song to spell the name of your road, town, county and so on.

SPELLING RECORDS

OBJECTIVE: to spell words with the common suffix 'ful'
LEARNING LINK: visual
ORGANISATION: pairs (teacher/adult-led); whole class
RESOURCES: sound recording equipment (a tape recorder or a computer with simple sound recording software – you may need to teach use of sound recording equipment before the activity); a list of six words, such as: 'helpful', 'painful', 'careful', 'mouthful', 'playful', 'restful', for each pair

WHAT TO DO

● Read out the words for your partner to spell out loud.
● Record everything that they say.
● Play the recording to the whole class.
● Ask them to listen to the words and how they are spelled.
● Are the spellings correct?
● If the spellings are incorrect, the rest of the class should suggest corrections.

NOW TRY THIS

Throughout the week, other pairs spell and record words that need practise, or a current topic word. Again, play the recordings to the rest of the class to check for accuracy.

SPONGE LETTERS ACTIVITY

OBJECTIVE: to sound and name each letter of the alphabet in lower case
LEARNING LINK: auditory, visual
ORGANISATION: individual
RESOURCES: paint in trays; newspaper; aprons; sponge lower-case letters; paper, for each child

WHAT TO DO

● Choose some sponge letters to print with on paper.
● Say the name of each letter and the sound it makes.
● Now press each sponge letter into paint and print it on paper.
● Look at the shape each letter makes.

NOW TRY THIS

See how many words you can print using the sponge letters. Ask a friend to read the words back to you. Have you spelled them correctly?

PLAYDOUGH PRACTICE

OBJECTIVE: to sound and name each letter of the alphabet in lower and upper case
LEARNING LINK: auditory, visual
ORGANISATION: individual
RESOURCES: playdough; paint in trays; newspaper; aprons, for each child

WHAT TO DO

● Make small (lower-case) letters out of playdough.
● Show them to the teacher and say each letter name and its sound.
● Now make capital letters in the same way.

NOW TRY THIS

Make your name using playdough letters. Make your first name and your last name. Paint the letters and put your name on the display table for everyone to see.

TRACING LETTERS

OBJECTIVE: to sound and name each letter of the alphabet in lower and upper case
LEARNING LINK: auditory
ORGANISATION: pairs
RESOURCES: none

WHAT TO DO

● Trace a small letter on your partner's back.
● Ask them to guess the letter name.
● If they are correct, give them a point.
● Now let them trace a small letter on your back.
● Guess what the letter is.
● If you are correct, your partner will give you one point.
● At the end of the session, see who has won the most points.

NOW TRY THIS

1. Play the game again, but this time trace capital letters on each other's backs.
2. Take turns to trace the name of a child in class on each other's backs. How many names can you guess correctly?
3. Take turns to trace the name of a teacher or helper on each other's backs. These are much harder to guess. How many can you get right? Remember to trace a capital 'M' for 'Miss', 'Mrs' and 'Mr'.

FEELY BAG GAME

OBJECTIVE: to secure knowledge of the letter sounds
LEARNING LINK: auditory, kinaesthetic
ORGANISATION: groups of three
RESOURCES: a cloth bag with a drawstring top; sets of large wooden letters (lower case) for each group

WHAT TO DO

- Place the letters in the bag and shake the bag to mix them up.
- Feel inside the bag for a letter. Don't remove the letter but feel its outline.
- Tell the group what the letter is and then say its sound.
- Now pull the letter out of the bag.
- Keep the letter if you sounded it out correctly; if not, return the letter to the bag.
- Pass the bag to another child in the group and repeat the activity until all the letters have been removed from the bag.
- The winner is the child with the most letters.

NOW TRY THIS

Use capital letters instead of small letters in the bag.

FORWARDS AND BACKWARDS

OBJECTIVE: to discriminate and segment all three phonemes in CVC words
LEARNING LINK: kinaesthetic, visual
ORGANISATION: individual
RESOURCES: ten words cut into individual letters, with the letters of each word paper clipped together, with the vowel in the medial position (each set of letters should make two words simply by reversing the initial and final letters, for example, 'pit /tip'; 'nap/pan'; 'ten/net'; 'tug/gut'; 'dog/god'; 'bad/dab'; 'nip/pin'; 'pot/top') for each child

WHAT TO DO

- Unclip the letters for a word.
- Spread the letters out.
- Make two words by swapping the first and last letters around.
- Write down the two words you have made.
- Continue with the next set of letters until you have done them all.

NOW TRY THIS

Choose one of the words you have made. See how many words you can think of using the same word family, for example, 'p*in* – t*in*', 'w*in*, d*in*'.

WORD FAMILIES

OBJECTIVE: to spell all three phonemes in CVC words, in rhyming and then non-rhyming sets
LEARNING LINK: visual
ORGANISATION: pairs
RESOURCES: letter tiles, for each pair

WHAT TO DO

- With your partner, use the letter tiles to make a rime (the end part of a syllable), for example, 'an'.
- Then add the first letter to make new words, for example, 'r*an*', 'c*an*', 'b*an*'.
- Say the words aloud. Notice how the words rhyme.
- Now choose a vowel only, for example 'e'.
- Choose different start and end letters to make lots of new words, such as, 'p*e*t', 'h*e*n', 'b*e*g'.
- How many non-rhyming, three-letter words can you make, using the same middle vowel?

NOW TRY THIS

How many rhyming words can you and your partner make, using the following rimes: 'ish', 'ash', 'uch', 'ath'?

TRACE THE SHAPE

OBJECTIVE: to practise forming letters correctly (lower-case letters only)
LEARNING LINK: auditory, kinaesthetic, visual
ORGANISATION: individual
RESOURCES: a set of hollow letters or letter templates, for each child

WHAT TO DO

- Look at each letter one at a time.
- Say the letter name and its sound aloud.
- With you finger, trace the letter shape.
- Make sure you make the correct sequence of movements to make the letter shape.

NOW TRY THIS

Try making simple two-letter words with the hollow letters, such as 'an', 'is', 'it' and 'on'. Trace your finger around each of the letters and then say the word.

TACTILE LEARNING

WEAVE A LETTER

OBJECTIVE: to practise forming letters correctly (upper-case letters only)
LEARNING LINK: kinaesthetic, visual
ORGANISATION: individual
RESOURCES: pegboard; pegs; wool, for each child

WHAT TO DO
• Place the pegs in the shape of the capital letter that you want to practise, for example, 'A'.
• Wind the wool round the pegs to make the letter.
• Make sure you wind the wool using the sequence of movements that you would use to write the letter.

NOW TRY THIS
1. Practise all the letters of the alphabet in this way.
2. Weave the initials of your name on the pegboard with the wool.

STRING LETTERS

OBJECTIVE: to practise forming letters correctly for writing
LEARNING LINK: tactile, visual
ORGANISATION: small groups of three or four
RESOURCES: pairs of scissors; 15–20 long pieces of thin string (test that the string is flexible and long enough for the children to shape into letters, before the activity) for each group

WHAT TO DO
• Imagine that the string is your pencil. Touch the tip of the string on the table so you are ready to 'write'.
• Now practise making a letter shape, using the string. Cut the string when you need to 'lift your pencil'. Remember to 'write' the letters using the correct sequence.
• Try to 'write' two more letters.
• When your group has finished, invite another group to sound all your letters out loud.

NOW TRY THIS
1. Use this activity to practise joining two letters together.
2. Blindfold your partner. Make a letter with the string. Ask your partner to feel the letter and guess its name.
3. Try writing short words using string to make each letter. Your blindfolded partner can feel the letters and guess the word.

LETTER SHAPES

OBJECTIVE: to practise forming letters in response to letter sounds
LEARNING LINK: auditory, visual
ORGANISATION: whole class, split into groups (teacher/adult-led)
RESOURCES: squares of gummed paper; scissors; thin card, for each group

WHAT TO DO
• The teacher will say a letter sound.
• Draw each letter on gummed paper, as a solid shape (no holes).
• Cut out each shape and then stick it on to card.
• At the end of the session, show some of your letters to the class and say each letter name and the sound it makes.

NOW TRY THIS
Make your name out of gummed paper and stick it on to card. Display your name for the class to see, at the end of the session.

SAND TRAY

OBJECTIVE: to practise forming letters correctly; to discriminate and segment all three phonemes in CVC words
LEARNING LINK: auditory, kinaesthetic, visual
ORGANISATION: pairs
RESOURCES: a tray of sand, for each pair

WHAT TO DO
• Take turns to write a three-letter word in the sand.
• Make sure you write each letter carefully, using the correct sequence of movements.
• Ask your partner to read the word aloud.
• Now swap and let your partner write a word in the sand for you to read.

NOW TRY THIS
Write the first sound and the last sound of a word, in the sand (leave a gap in between them). Ask your partner to add a middle letter to make a word. Now swap and ask your partner to write the first and last sounds for you to fill in the missing letter.

WORD BAG FUN

OBJECTIVE: to secure understanding of the terms 'vowel' and 'consonant'
LEARNING LINK: visual
ORGANISATION: small groups
RESOURCES: two cloth bags – one containing vowel letter tiles, the other containing consonants (select the letters carefully so that CVC words can be made easily) for each group

WHAT TO DO

● Take turns to pick out one vowel letter tile and two consonant letter tiles.
● Try and make three-letter words using the tiles.
● Say the word you have made.
● Return the tiles to the bag and shake the bag well.
● Continue until everyone has had a turn at making three-letter words.

NOW TRY THIS

Place all the tiles in the bag. Take turns to pull out a letter and say if it is a vowel or a consonant.

Award a point for every correct answer. Add up the points to find the winner.

TESSELLATING TANGLES

OBJECTIVE: to read and spell words with initial consonant clusters through blending
LEARNING LINK: visual
ORGANISATION: individual
RESOURCES: tessellating word cards cut out from photocopiable page 62; pencils and paper, for each child

WHAT TO DO

● Spread the cards out on the table.
● See how many words you can make by fitting the cards together.
● Write the words on to paper as you make them.

NOW TRY THIS

Use the start consonant clusters to make more words. How many new words can you make?

GLUE AND GLITTER WORDS

OBJECTIVE: to discriminate, read and spell words with initial consonant clusters, for example 'gl'
LEARNING LINK: visual
ORGANISATION: individual
RESOURCES: glue in pots; glue brush; glitter; paper, for each child

WHAT TO DO

● Write 'gl' words on your paper for example, 'glad', 'glum', 'glue', 'glen', 'glass', using the glue and glue brush.
● Sprinkle the glitter over the glue. (The glitter will stick to the glue to make the words glitter.)
● See how many glittery 'gl' words you can make.

NOW TRY THIS

In pairs, think of a secret message to send to your partner that includes some 'gl' words, for example, *The glue is by the glass.* Take turns to write your message on the paper with the glue and glue brush. Ask your partner to sprinkle glitter over the words to reveal the secret message!

POTATO LETTERS

OBJECTIVE: to discriminate onset from rime in speech and spelling
LEARNING LINK: visual
ORGANISATION: groups
RESOURCES: a series of individual letter stamps cut out of potatoes (letters for CVC words); paint in trays; newspaper; aprons; paper; felt-tipped pens, for each group

WHAT TO DO

● The teacher will give your group a rime (the end part of a syllable), for example, 'an'.
● Write the rime on a piece of paper using felt-tipped pens.
● Choose an onset (the start of a syllable) from the potato stamps.
● Now dip the potato stamp in paint and print it next to the rime, for example, add 'r' to 'an' to make '*r*an' or 'p' to 'an' to make '*p*an'.
● At the end of the session, show the words you have made to the rest of the class.
● Read the words aloud to other children in your group.

NOW TRY THIS

Hold a contest to see who can make the longest list of words that have the same spelling pattern.

TACTILE LEARNING

COMPUTER SPELL TIME

OBJECTIVE: to secure phonemic spelling
LEARNING LINK: visual
ORGANISATION: individual
RESOURCES: access to a computer; a list of ten words, for example, high frequency words or words containing long vowel phonemes, for each child

WHAT TO DO

● The teacher will give you a list of spellings. Read each word carefully.
● At your computer, open the word processing program and type in all of your words.
● Try out different fonts, sizes and colours. See how many different ways you can write the words.
● Check your spellings against the spelling list to make sure that you have spelled them correctly.

NOW TRY THIS

When you have finished, print out your work so that it can be put on display for others to see.

SNAP!

OBJECTIVE: to learn common spelling patterns for vowel phoneme 'oo' (short, as in 'good') and 'ar', 'oy', 'ow'
LEARNING LINK: auditory, kinaesthetic, visual
ORGANISATION: pairs
RESOURCES: a set of 12 word cards as follows: 'good', 'hood', 'stood', 'wood', 'car', 'tar', 'star', 'far', 'boy', 'toy', 'cow', 'now', for each pair

WHAT TO DO

● Shuffle the cards and divide them into two equal piles; take one pile each.
● Hold your cards, in your hand, face down.
● Now, each of you places one card, face up on the table.
● If the vowel sounds in each word are the same, say *Snap!*
● The first child to say *Snap!* keeps the pair of cards.
● Play the game until no more pairs can be found.

NOW TRY THIS

Use the cards to test each other's spelling. Ask your partner to read the words to you one at a time. Spell the words aloud. Give points for each correct spelling. Now swap and you test your partner's spelling. Who spelled the most words correctly?

WORD PUZZLE

OBJECTIVE: to discriminate, read and spell spelling patterns for long vowel phoneme 'or'
LEARNING LINK: kinaesthetic, visual
ORGANISATION: pairs
RESOURCES: ten word cards (cut each word into three phoneme strips, for example, 'sp–or–t', and paper clip them together) – suggested words: 'sport', 'floor', 'claw', 'bought', 'more', 'store', 'door', 'draw', 'thought', 'caught', for each pair

WHAT TO DO

● Unclip each set of cards, one at a time.
● Ask your partner to sort the cards so they spell a word with a long vowel sound.
● Now cover the word with your hand.
● Challenge your partner to spell the word aloud.
● Check that the spelling is right.
● Swap roles and repeat the activity.

NOW TRY THIS

Play the game again, but this time, ask your partner to think up a sentence, using the word spelled.

THREAD A WORD

OBJECTIVE: to discriminate, read and spell the common spelling patterns for vowel phoneme 'air'
LEARNING LINK: kinaesthetic, visual
ORGANISATION: pairs
RESOURCES: small squares of thin card with a letter on each (paper clipped together so each group of letters forms a word – suggested words: 'hair', 'share', 'scare', 'there', 'bear', 'where', 'wear', 'fair', 'fare', stare); thin wool; large-eyed needles, for each pair

WHAT TO DO

● Unclip the set of letters on your table, one at a time.
● Put the letters into the right order.
● Thread the words together using the needle and wool.

NOW TRY THIS

1. Make a necklace or bracelet to wear with your name on it. Write your name on to pieces of card (one letter for each piece of card). Thread the letters in the right order using the needle and wool.
2. Thread a message on to your necklace, for example; 'Mia is fun'. Put a plain piece of card between each word to split them up.

WORD SORTING

OBJECTIVE: to secure phonemic spelling
LEARNING LINK: visual
ORGANISATION: individual
RESOURCES: 20 playing cards as follows: 'pair', 'stair', 'thaw', 'straw', 'good', 'stood', 'far', 'car', 'cow', 'how', 'find', 'kind', 'feet', 'meet', 'train', 'stain', 'high', 'sigh', 'play', 'day', for each child

WHAT TO DO
- Shuffle the cards.
- Turn the cards over, one at a time, and place them on the table.
- Look carefully at the spelling patterns.
- If two words have the same spelling pattern, put them together.
- Continue until all the cards have been placed into their word pairs.

NOW TRY THIS
1. Ask a partner to test your spellings using the word cards. How many did you get right? Practise spelling the words that you found difficult.
2. How fast can you spell the words? See how many words you can spell in one minute.
3. Play the 'Word sorting' game again, but this time, see if you can think of an additional word to rhyme with each pair, for example, 'stair'... 'fair'.

LETTER TILES

OBJECTIVE: to split words into phonemes for spelling
LEARNING LINK: kinaesthetic, visual
ORGANISATION: pairs
RESOURCES: sets of letter tiles, for each pair

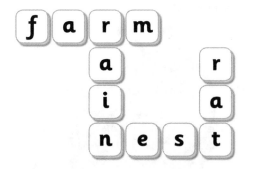

WHAT TO DO
- Place the tiles face down on the table.
- Share the letter tiles between you.

- Stand your letter tiles up so that only you can see them.
- Ask your partner to try and make a word using their own tiles.
- Now see if you can make a word with your tiles by using one of your partner's letter tiles as a start sound.
- If you cannot, you have to miss a turn.
- Continue until all the tiles have been used up or you cannot continue playing.

NOW TRY THIS
Look at the words you have made. Who has made the longest word? What was it? How many letters did it have? Play the game again and see if you can make an even longer word than last time.

COLOURING WORD FAMILIES

OBJECTIVE: to recognise words by common spelling patterns
LEARNING LINK: visual
ORGANISATION: individual
RESOURCES: prepared worksheets (as suggested below); colouring pencils/felt-tipped pens, for each child

WHAT TO DO
- Look at the words on the sheet.
- Read them to yourself.
- Look carefully at the word endings.
- Colour 'ill' words in red. Colour 'ell' words in green. Colour 'ull' words in yellow.

NOW TRY THIS
How many more 'ill', 'ell' or 'ull' words can you think of? Write them on the back of your sheet.

STRAW WORDS

OBJECTIVE: to segment words into phonemes for spelling

LEARNING LINK: visual

ORGANISATION: individual

RESOURCES: a list of words written on the board, linked to a current project, for example, 'My body'; glue; sugar paper; paper straws cut into pieces, for each child

WHAT TO DO

● Look at the words on the board.

● Choose three words you would like to spell.

● Make the words by shaping the letters out of straws.

● Stick the straw letters on to the sugar paper in the right order.

● Check your spellings carefully.

NOW TRY THIS

Ask a partner to test you to see if you can spell from memory the words you have made.

LET'S SEW

OBJECTIVE: to segment words into phonemes for spelling

LEARNING LINK: visual

ORGANISATION: individual

RESOURCES: a list of words with a long vowel phoneme, for example, for 'oa': 'boat', 'coat', 'goat'; pieces of binca; large-eyed needles; coloured thread; pencils, for each child

WHAT TO DO

● Look at the list of words on the board.

● Decide which word you want to illustrate, for example 'a boat'.

● Draw an outline of your picture on the binca using a pencil.

● Sew on top of the outline using running stitch.

● Draw a label for your picture on the binca, using a pencil, for example 'b-o-a-t'.

● Sew on top of each letter using running stitch.

● Sew your initials to the bottom of your picture to show whose work it is.

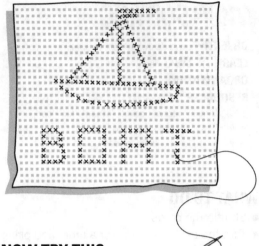

NOW TRY THIS

Work as a group to sew a sentence for display.

CANDLES AND CRAYONS

OBJECTIVE: to segment words into phonemes for spelling

LEARNING LINK: visual

ORGANISATION: individual, small groups or whole class

RESOURCES: white wax candles; crayons; paper, for each child

WHAT TO DO

● Think of a word containing a spelling pattern, for example, 'nd' endings.

● Write the word in candle wax on your paper.

● Swap papers with your partner.

● Crayon over the wax to reveal the word.

● Did you both spell your word correctly?

● How many different 'nd' words did the class think of, altogether?

NOW TRY THIS

Make up secret messages using the candle wax to write your message. Swap papers and crayon over the wax to find out what the secret messages are!

WORD WALL GAME

OBJECTIVE: to recognise critical features of words: length
LEARNING LINK: visual
ORGANISATION: pairs
RESOURCES: sets of letter tiles, for each pair.

WHAT TO DO
- Spread the letter tiles face up on the table
- The first player makes a word using two letters, for example, 'an'.
- Now take turns to add more letters to build a longer word and make a wall. Each time you add a letter it must make a new word, for example, 'an – and'; 'sand – sandy'.
- If you can't go, say *pass*. The player who adds the most letters to the wall is the winner.

NOW TRY THIS
Work with your partner against the clock. See how long a word wall you can make in one minute using the start word 'up'.

WHOSE NAME?

OBJECTIVE: to recognise the critical features of words: shape
LEARNING LINK: visual
ORGANISATION: whole class
RESOURCES: a box; pieces of A5 paper; paper clips; A5 red and yellow thin card; scissors; pencils, for each child

WHAT TO DO
- Attach a piece of paper with paper clips to a piece of card (red for girls and yellow for boys). Write your name on the paper.
- Cut around the paper and the card to make a name shape.
- Now give the paper shape to the teacher.
- Put the card shape in a box.
- One at a time, pick a shape out of the box and guess whose name shape it is.
- Check to see if you are right by placing their paper name shape on top of the card to see if it fits.
- Repeat until all the names have been picked.

NOW TRY THIS
Play the game using names of teaching staff.

SPLITTING UP

OBJECTIVE: to discriminate orally the syllables in multi-syllabic words
LEARNING LINK: visual
ORGANISATION: individual
RESOURCES: scissors; ten word cards showing compound words as follows: 'himself', 'milkman', 'pancake', 'teaspoon', 'windscreen, 'headache', 'ladybird', 'chalkboard', 'eggcup', 'football', for each child

WHAT TO DO
- Look at each compound word card.
- Read the word to yourself.
- Decide where to cut the word to make two smaller words.
- Cut the word into two.
- Place the two words together on the table.
- Repeat this until you have split all the compound words into two parts.

NOW TRY THIS
See if you can make some more compound words from the parts that you have cut up, for example, 'headboard' or 'teacup'.

MAGNETIC MAGIC

OBJECTIVE: to investigate and learn spellings of verbs with 'ed' and 'ing' endings
LEARNING LINK: auditory, visual
ORGANISATION: small groups
RESOURCES: magnetic letters; magnetic boards; list of words, for example: 'jumped', 'skipped', 'laughed', 'sniffed', 'lifted', 'walked', 'talked', 'wanted', 'needed', 'helped', for each group

WHAT TO DO
- Using the magnetic letters, take turns to spell a word from the list.
- Check each other's spellings.
- Say each word aloud as a group. Does each word have a 't' or 'd' sound at the end?
- Remember that words ending in 'ed' can sound like there is 't' at the end.
- Play the game until all the words on the list have been spelled.

NOW TRY THIS
Now think of your own verbs ending in 'ing'.

MATCHING TRIANGLES

OBJECTIVE: to spell words with prefixes 'un' and 'dis'
LEARNING LINK: kinaesthetic, visual
ORGANISATION: individual
RESOURCES: triangular word cards (see below) using 'un' or 'dis' prefixes – suggested words as follows: 'undo', 'undress', 'uneven', 'unfair', 'unhealthy', 'dislike', 'disown', 'displease', 'disappear', for each child

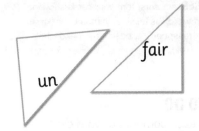

WHAT TO DO

- Spread the triangles out on the table.
- Decide which words sound correct when either 'un' or 'dis' is placed in front of them.
- Put the triangles together to make words.
- Read your words to the teacher.

NOW TRY THIS

How many other 'un' or 'dis' words can you think of? Make a list on a whiteboard.

RHYMING PAIRS

OBJECTIVE: to investigate and classify words which have the same sound but different spellings
LEARNING LINK: kinaesthetic, visual
ORGANISATION: pairs
RESOURCES: ten cards to make five pairs of homophones (for example: 'stair', 'stare', 'hair', 'hare', 'bear', 'bare', 'their', 'there', 'wear', 'where') for each pair

WHAT TO DO

- Shuffle the cards and place them face down on the table.
- Take turns to turn over two cards.
- If the cards sound exactly the same, keep the pair.
- If they do not match, return them to the pack.
- The winner is the child with the most pairs at the end of the game.

NOW TRY THIS

Play the game again. If you turn over words with the same sound, you may keep the pair only if you can explain the meanings of both words.

WORD MAZE

OBJECTIVE: to split compound words into their component parts
LEARNING LINK: visual
ORGANISATION: whole class
RESOURCES: a copy of photocopiable page 63; colouring pencils, for each child

WHAT TO DO

- Read the words at the top of the page.
- Read the words at the bottom.
- Using a colouring pencil, trace over each line, starting from a top word, to find its partner.
- Write the compound word in the space provided.

NOW TRY THIS

On a fresh sheet of paper, make up your own word maze of compound words. Give the sheet to your partner for them to solve. How many words did they get right?

ANIMAL SORTING

OBJECTIVE: to collect new words of personal interest or words linked to particular topics
LEARNING LINK: kinaesthetic, visual
ORGANISATION: individual
RESOURCES: a set of envelopes each containing a zoo animal name card (each name card should be cut into individual letters); small whiteboards; dry-wipe markers, for each child

WHAT TO DO

- Tip the letters out of the animal envelope.
- Place the letters in the right order to spell an animal's name.
- Write the animal's name on your whiteboard.
- If you are right, choose another animal envelope to work out.

NOW TRY THIS

Make your own animal puzzle for a partner to work out.

ZIGZAG

OBJECTIVE: to collect new words linked to particular topics
LEARNING LINK: visual
ORGANISATION: pairs
RESOURCES: A4 paper and pencil, for each child (demonstrate how to fold pieces of paper into concertina shapes and how to write one letter of a word on each fold)

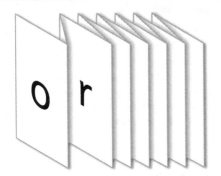

WHAT TO DO
● Fold your paper into a concertina shape.
● Write the name of a fruit on to the concertina. Write one letter on each fold.
● Hand the folded concertina to your partner.
● See how many letters they have to unfold before they can work out the name of the fruit.
● Who solved the puzzle using the fewest number of letters?

NOW TRY THIS
Choose another topic, for example, 'colours'. Write the letters of a colour on the concertina, as before. This time, ask your partner to solve the puzzle by working backwards. How many letters did they need to see before they could work out the answer?

WEATHER WORDS

OBJECTIVE: to collect new words linked to particular topics
LEARNING LINK: auditory, visual
ORGANISATION: small groups
RESOURCES: various paints; newspaper; aprons; large pieces of coloured sugar paper, for each group

WHAT TO DO
● Spread your piece of sugar paper out on the table.
● In your group, talk about interesting ways to paint weather words, for example, 'rain' could be painted so that each letter is the shape of a raindrop. Think about colours, lines and shape.

● Decide between you, who will paint which weather type. Choose from 'rain', 'snow', 'hail', 'wind', 'thunder', 'lightning', 'sun', 'cloudy'.
● Write your words, in paint, on the sugar paper.
● At the end of the session, take turns to show your weather word to the rest of your group.
● Ask the others to check that you have spelled your word correctly.

NOW TRY THIS
Make a large class weather chart. Fill in the weather every day, using the words made during the group work (you will need to cut the words out).

CUT OUT AND SPELL

OBJECTIVE: to collect new words from reading, linked to particular topics
LEARNING LINK: kinaesthetic, visual
ORGANISATION: pairs
RESOURCES: a wordbank linked to a particular topic; strips of paper; pencils; scissors; envelopes, for each child

WHAT TO DO
● Work in pairs.
● Choose a word from the list and write it on to a strip of paper.
● Cut the word into letters and put the letters into an envelope.
● Swap envelopes with your partner.
● See if you can work out your partner's word.
● Play again, this time, choosing a different word from the list.
● How many words did you spell correctly?

NOW TRY THIS
1. Choose another topic that you are working on in school, for example, 'My body'. Make word puzzles with words from this topic for other groups to solve.
2. Play the game again, but this time, spell numbers zero to twenty.

PASTA FUN

OBJECTIVE: to spell names of classroom objects and label them accurately
LEARNING LINK: visual
ORGANISATION: pairs
RESOURCES: classroom objects; pasta shapes; glue; strips of card, for each pair

WHAT TO DO

● Decide which classroom object you and your partner are going to label.
● Make sure you can spell the word. Use a dictionary if you are unsure.
● Make the label using pasta shapes to form each letter.
● Stick the pasta shape letters on to the card in the right order.
● Place your label next to the object.

NOW TRY THIS

Have more pasta shape fun by making your name out of pasta shapes. Paint the pasta to make your name look even more special!

FLOWER WORDS

OBJECTIVE: to collect words linked to particular topics.
LEARNING LINK: visual
ORGANISATION: individual
RESOURCES: flower shapes on paper (as shown below) including petals to cut out and stick to the flower centre – each petal has a letter on it to make the name of one flower, for example: 'daisy', 'rose', 'pansy', 'lupin'; scissors; colouring pencils; glue, for each child

WHAT TO DO

● Cut out the petals on your paper.
● Sort the letters to make the name of the flower.
● Glue the petals from left to right around the flower head.
● Colour the flower head and stalk.

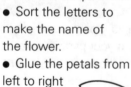
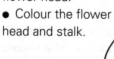
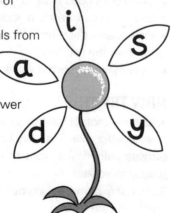

NOW TRY THIS

Make your own flower word puzzle for a partner to put together. Try to make longer and more difficult flower names, such as buttercup, dandelion.

WASHING LINE

OBJECTIVE: to secure knowledge of alphabetical order
LEARNING LINK: visual
ORGANISATION: whole class
RESOURCES: a piece of string hung across a wall; small pegs; 26 words each beginning with a different letter of the alphabet – suggested words: 'and', 'big', 'cat', 'dad', 'egg', 'for', 'got', 'his', 'if', 'jam', 'kit', 'lad', 'mum', 'not', 'on', 'put', 'queen', 'ran', 'saw', 'too', 'us', 'van', 'we', 'x-ray', 'yes', 'zoo'

WHAT TO DO

● Look at each word. Look at the first letter of each word.
● Sort the words into alphabetical order.
● Peg the words up on the line in alphabetical order.
● As a class, check that you have pegged the words up correctly.

NOW TRY THIS

1. Take turns to work against the clock to see how fast you can peg the words up in the correct order. Ask your partner to start the stopwatch. Stop the clock as soon as you have pegged up the last word. How long did it take you? Now swap roles and you time your partner.
2. Make this game much harder by pegging the words up in reverse alphabetical order, starting with 'zoo'. Check that you have pegged the words in the correct order.
3. Repeat the activity above, against the clock. Who can complete the task the fastest? How long did they take?

MISSING LETTERS

OBJECTIVE: to spell the days of the week
LEARNING LINK: kinaesthetic, visual
ORGANISATION: individual
RESOURCES: sets of cards with days of the week written on them, each with two or three letters missing, as follows: 'M–d-y', 'T–s-a y', 'W-dn-s–y', 'T-ur-day', 'F–day', 'S-t-rd-y', '-un-ay'; provide the missing letters on individual cards; glue, for each child

WHAT TO DO
- Look at the days of the week cards carefully.
- Work out the missing letters.
- Stick the missing letters on each card in the right spaces.
- Show your finished work to the teacher.

NOW TRY THIS
Place the days of the week in the right order, beginning with Monday. Which days are at the weekend?

DAYS OF THE WEEK MUDDLE

OBJECTIVE: to spell the days of the week
LEARNING LINK: visual
ORGANISATION: individual
RESOURCES: letter cards for the names of the days of the week; a small whiteboard, for each child

WHAT TO DO
- Spread out the letters for all the days of the week.
- Find the letters for the first day of the week–Monday.
- Place the letters for this day at the top of your whiteboard. Make sure you place them in the right order.
- Continue spelling the days of the week until you have finished.
- Check that the days are in the right order.

NOW TRY THIS
Draw a picture about your favourite day of the week. Write a sentence to say why it is your favourite day, for example; *My favourite day is Monday because that is when I go swimming.*

RAINBOW YEAR

OBJECTIVE: to spell the months of the year
LEARNING LINK: kinaesthetic, visual
ORGANISATION: whole class, split into four groups
RESOURCES: sets of wooden letters (upper and lower case); colouring pencils or felt-tipped pens; large sheets of sugar paper, for each group

WHAT TO DO
- The teacher tells your group the names of months from a season, for example, for spring: 'March', 'April', 'May'.
- Talk about the colours that reflect the season.
- Write the months' names you have been given by tracing around the wooden letters on your table.
- Remember to begin each month with a capital letter.
- Colour the letters to reflect the season, for example, browns, yellows and dark reds for autumn.
- At the end of the session, show the others your group's work.

NOW TRY THIS
1. Repeat the activity for the names of the seasons. Use these as headings for a wall display.
2. Use the wooden letters to trace around your birthday month. Decorate the letters with all the special things that remind you of your birthday, such as presents, cards and so on. When you have finished ask the teacher to laminate your work so that you can display it at home.

KINAESTHETIC LEARNING

WALK THE LETTERS

OBJECTIVE: to practise forming letters correctly for writing

LEARNING LINK: tactile, visual

ORGANISATION: small groups or whole class

RESOURCES: lower-case letters of the alphabet (not 'i', 't' or 'x') written on a hall floor, using coloured floor chalks

WHAT TO DO

● Pretend your feet are a pencil.

● Walk on the letters to draw them with your feet. Make sure you travel in the right direction!

NOW TRY THIS

Repeat the activity using capital letters. Jump in the air to show where you lift your pencil off the page, for example, in letters 'A' and 'T'.

WALK THE WORDS

OBJECTIVE: to practise forming letters correctly for writing

LEARNING LINK: auditory, tactile, visual

ORGANISATION: small groups or whole class

RESOURCES: a selection of CVC words written on a hall floor (in lower case) using coloured floor chalks

WHAT TO DO

● Pretend your feet are a pencil.

● Walk on the words to draw them with your feet. Make sure you travel in the right direction!

● Tell the teacher what the word says before you move on to the next word.

NOW TRY THIS

1. Repeat the activity for longer words.

2. Take turns to walk a friend's name.

3. Make this activity even harder by walking a short message for your friends. Clap your hands to show the start of each new word.

WHAT LETTER AM I?

OBJECTIVE: to practise forming letters correctly for writing

LEARNING LINK: –

ORGANISATION: whole class, in groups of three

RESOURCES: a hall; mats

WHAT TO DO

● Make a capital letter shape using your bodies (lie on the floor if this is easier).

● The other children guess what the letter is.

● The child who guesses correctly is the next person to make a capital letter, with their group.

● Play the game until all the capital letters have been attempted.

NOW TRY THIS

Work in groups of five to try to spell a CVC word. The other groups must try to guess your word.

AIR WRITING

OBJECTIVE: to practise forming letters correctly for writing
LEARNING LINK: visual
ORGANISATION: whole class
RESOURCES: none

WHAT TO DO

- The teacher stands with their back to you and draws a letter in the air.
- Copy the movements and tell the teacher what the letter is.
- Practise capital and small letters.

NOW TRY THIS

Working in pairs, take turns to write a letter in the air for your partner to guess. Remember to stand with your back to your partner when you write each letter.

AIR WORDS

OBJECTIVES: to write letters in the air, using the correct formation; to blend phonemes for spelling
LEARNING LINK: visual
ORGANISATION: whole class
RESOURCES: none

WHAT TO DO

- The teacher stands with their back to the group and writes a word in the air.
- Guess what the word is.
- The teacher writes more words, with same spelling pattern.
- Remember to blend the letter sounds to help you read the words.

NOW TRY THIS

Working in pairs, take turns to write a word with the same spelling pattern in the air for your partner to read.

ROPE WORDS

OBJECTIVES: to write letters using the correct sequence of movements; to spell CVC words
LEARNING LINK: tactile; visual
ORGANISATION: small groups
RESOURCES: scissors; 30 or more long pieces of thin string (test that the string is flexible and long enough for the children to shape into letters, before the activity) for each group

WHAT TO DO

- Imagine that the string is your pencil. Touch the tip of the string on the table so you are ready to 'write'.
- Use the string to 'write' three-letter words, for example, 'cat'. Cut the string when you need to 'lift your pencil'.
- Remember to 'write' the letters using the correct sequence.
- Invite other groups to see your words and read what they say.

NOW TRY THIS

1. Use this activity to practise joining letters in short words
2. 'Write' words with vowel sounds ai; ou; or.

TALL, TINY AND TAILS

OBJECTIVE: to practise forming lower-case letters correctly, for joining
LEARNING LINK: auditory, visual
ORGANISATION: whole class
RESOURCES: PE benches representing handwriting lines, placed around a hall; mats; use flash cards to check that the children can recognise all letter names, before the activity.

WHAT TO DO

- Imagine that each bench is a line on a piece of paper.
- The teacher calls a letter of the alphabet. For
  - 'Letters with sticks!' – stand on a bench and stretch your arms above your head;
  - 'Letters with no sticks!' – sit on a bench with your legs crossed;
  - 'Letters with tails!' – sit on a bench and let your feet hang down.
- Play the game until all the letters have been practised.

NOW TRY THIS

Speed up this game to see who is caught out!

KINAESTHETIC LEARNING

LETTER MOVEMENTS

OBJECTIVE: to recall the sounds for the letters of the alphabet
LEARNING LINK: auditory, visual
ORGANISATION: whole class
RESOURCES: a stack of lower-case letter flash cards

WHAT TO DO

- Look at the letter cards, one at a time.
- Think of a good action for each letter, for example, making a snake movement for 's'.
- Put your hand up when you have thought of an idea. The teacher will decide which actions to use for each letter.
- When you are shown the letters cards again, do the chosen movements.

NOW TRY THIS

Play the game again, but this time as quickly as possible. How many children were caught out? How many kept up the pace?

RUN FOR IT!

OBJECTIVE: to identify initial phonemes in words
LEARNING LINK: auditory
ORGANISATION: whole class
RESOURCES: a hall; two large letter cards – one showing the letter 'b' the other 'd'; suggested list of words: 'big', 'dad', 'bad', 'dog', 'dig', 'den', 'but', 'by', 'din', 'bat'

WHAT TO DO

- The teacher asks two children to stand at one end of the hall and hold up the letter cards.
- The teacher says a word beginning with either 'b' or 'd'.
- If the word begins with 'b', run and stand behind the child holding the 'b' card. If the word begins with 'd', run and stand behind the child holding the 'd' card.
- Children who choose the right card will stay in the game.
- Children who get it wrong must sit out.

NOW TRY THIS

1. Make this game harder by adding some red herrings, that is, words that do not begin with 'b' or 'd'. If the teacher calls out one of these words, you must stand still. Anyone who makes the wrong movement will be out.
2. Play the game again, but this time, the teacher will say words beginning with 'b', 'd' and 'p'.

TWISTER

OBJECTIVE: to identify initial phonemes in words
LEARNING LINK: auditory, visual
ORGANISATION: whole class
RESOURCES: a blindfold; large letter cards placed in a large circle, in a hall

WHAT TO DO

- Sit in the class circle, on the floor, behind a letter.
- One child is blindfolded and stands in the middle of the circle of letters. The teacher turns the child around, two or three times.
- The blindfold is removed. The child is facing one of the letters.
- The child has to think of a word beginning with that letter.

NOW TRY THIS

Make the game harder by asking a child to think of a word that ends with their letter.

SPIN THE WHEEL

OBJECTIVE: to identify initial phonemes in words
LEARNING LINK: auditory, visual
ORGANISATION: whole class, sitting in a circle
RESOURCES: a large spinner with an arrow or pointer; letter flash cards, for each child

WHAT TO DO

- Each child holds a letter card.
- A spinner is placed in the middle of the circle.
- The teacher chooses one child to spin the spinner.
- When the spinner stops, the teacher calls out a category, such as *animals*.
- The child who is sitting in front of the spinner's pointer must think of an animal whose name starts with the letter on their card.
- If correct, this child is next to spin the spinner.

NOW TRY THIS

1. Make the game harder by asking a child to think of an animal that ends with their letter.
2. Try this really hard game. Spin the spinner twice. Your partner must think of a word that begins with the first letter and ends with the second letter that you have spun, for example, 'c', 'd'... 'card'.
3. Spin the spinner once. Your partner must think of a word that has that letter as a middle sound.

'SH' AND 'CH' GAME

OBJECTIVE: to identify initial phonemes in words
LEARNING LINK: auditory
ORGANISATION: small groups or whole class, in a large space
RESOURCES: a hall or playground

WHAT TO DO

● The teacher stands in front of you in the hall or playground and says words starting with 'sh' or 'ch'.
● If you hear a 'sh' sound, put your fingers to your lips and say *sh*. If you hear a 'ch' sound, move your arms like a steam train and say *ch, ch*!
● Children who make the wrong sound should sit out.

NOW TRY THIS

● Make this game harder by adding some red herrings, that is, words that do not begin with 'sh' or 'ch'. If the teacher calls out one of these words, you must stand still.
● Anyone who makes the wrong movement will be out.

SEMAPHORE

OBJECTIVE: to secure spelling of initial, final and medial letter sounds in CVC words
LEARNING LINK: visual
ORGANISATION: small groups
RESOURCES: two flags (show the children how to use semaphore, for the first ten letters of the alphabet only) for each group

WHAT TO DO

● Practise the semaphore movements for the first ten letters of the alphabet.
● Take turns to use the flags to spell three-letter words.
● Ask the others to work out your words.
● Award a point for every correct answer.
● Who guessed the most words correctly?

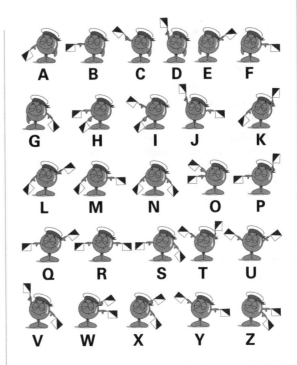

NOW TRY THIS

1. Learn more semaphore movements to help you to spell longer words.

GIANT PAIRS GAME

OBJECTIVES: to read initial, final and medial phonemes in simple words; to discriminate, blend common consonant clusters
LEARNING LINK: auditory, tactile, visual
ORGANISATION: small groups, in the hall
RESOURCES: a set of 20 large word cards (each set of cards should have ten pairs of matching words, as follows: 'help/help', 'stand/stand', 'wilt/wilt', 'ask/ask', 'crisp/crisp', 'blink/blink', 'limp/limp', 'fact/fact', 'next/next', 'stop/stop'); a hall partitioned into sections, for each group

WHAT TO DO

● Shuffle the cards.
● Place all 20 cards face down, on the floor, in your area of the hall.
● Take turns to move round the space and turn over two cards.
● If the cards match, keep the pair.
● If they do not match, let the next person in your group have a turn.
● The winner is the person with the most pairs of cards.

NOW TRY THIS

Shuffle the cards. Choose a child to read aloud the cards, making sure that no one else can see the words. Take turns to spell the words. Award one point for each correct answer. The winner is the child with the most points.

WAVE AND HOP GAME

OBJECTIVE: to discriminate and identify initial consonant clusters 'fl' and 'fr' in words

LEARNING LINK: auditory, visual

ORGANISATION: small groups, in the hall

RESOURCES: small paper flags for each child; a list of 'fl' and 'fr' words as follows: 'flag', 'frog', 'flap', 'fly', 'Friday', 'from', 'friend', 'fruit', 'flick', 'freeze', for each group

WHAT TO DO

- Find a space in the hall.
- Hold your flag by your side.
- Choose a child to read out the list of 'fl' and 'fr' words.
- After each word, wave your flag for the words that begin with 'fl', and hop like a frog for words beginning with 'fr'.
- Anyone who makes the wrong movement is out.
- Continue until all the words on the list have been read.

NOW TRY THIS

1. Think of more 'fl' and 'fr' words. Read them more quickly than before, and see how many people you can catch out!

2. Make this game even harder by spelling the words out loud as you wave or hop.

CONSONANT CLUSTER CIRCLES

OBJECTIVE: to discriminate initial consonant clusters in words

LEARNING LINK: auditory

ORGANISATION: whole class, in the hall

RESOURCES: a hall; large circles spread around the hall and drawn on the floor using floor chalk (in each circle, write the consonant cluster you wish to address, for example, 'bl', 'tr', 'cl', 'fr', 'gr'); a list of words: 'black', 'blue', 'clothes', 'brought', 'friends', 'great', 'brother'

WHAT TO DO

- Listen as the teacher reads out each word.
- Run and stand in the chalk circle that has the same start sound as that word.
- Earn one point if you chose correctly.
- The winner is the person with the most points.

NOW TRY THIS

1. Include a few red herrings in the list, for example, words with clusters that are not in any of the circles. Stand still if you hear a word that starts with a cluster that is not in the circles. If you move at all, you lose a point!

2. Play the game using words with three-letter clusters, for example, square, through, split.

PAT AND SPELL

OBJECTIVES: to discriminate final phonemes and consonant clusters in words; to spell words containing final consonant clusters correctly

LEARNING LINK: auditory

ORGANISATION: groups of six (teacher/adult-led)

RESOURCES: a balloon; a list of words with final consonant clusters: 'back', 'help', 'just', 'sent', 'went', 'jump', 'next', 'must', 'dust', 'wind', 'rust', 'self', 'fact', for each group

WHAT TO DO

- The teacher pats the balloon to a child and gives them a word to spell.
- Pat the balloon, to keep it in the air, while spelling the word.
- A point is scored for each correct spelling.
- The winner is the child with the most points.

NOW TRY THIS

As a group, choose a word and then pat the balloon around the circle. On your turn, say the next letter in the word. Play until the whole word has been spelled out correctly.

JUMP AND CLAP

OBJECTIVES: to discriminate and identify initial and final phonemes and consonant clusters in words
LEARNING LINK: auditory, visual
ORGANISATION: whole class; small groups
RESOURCES: a short story as shown below

<u>Cl</u>ive was very <u>cl</u>ever. He could ju<u>mp</u> very high. He could ju<u>mp</u> over a ra<u>mp</u>. He could ju<u>mp</u> over a stu<u>mp</u>.

'I'm so <u>cl</u>ever!' said <u>Cl</u>ive.

One day, <u>Cl</u>ive had a <u>cl</u>ever idea.

'I will make a big wall with a <u>cl</u>u<u>mp</u> of grass and a lu<u>mp</u> of mud. Then, I will ju<u>mp</u> over it!'

<u>Cl</u>ever <u>Cl</u>ive built the wall. Then he took a run and a ju<u>mp</u>. But he didn't ju<u>mp</u> over the wall at all. His ju<u>mp</u> was too low and he just crashed into it – BU<u>MP</u>! He got covered in the <u>cl</u>u<u>mp</u> of grass, and a lu<u>mp</u> of mud landed on his head!

'I'm not so <u>cl</u>ever now.' said <u>Cl</u>ive, sadly.

WHAT TO DO

● Listen to the story, 'Clever Clive'.
● If you hear words beginning with 'cl', clap once.
● If you hear words ending with 'mp', jump once in the air. If you hear a word beginning with 'cl' and ending with 'mp', jump and clap at the same time!

NOW TRY THIS

1. Make up a short story with 'st' start sounds and 'ck' end sounds. Tell the children in your group to stamp their feet once when they hear the 'st' start sound, and click their fingers if they hear the 'ck' end sound.
2. For an even harder game make up a story using words with 'cl', 'mp', 'st' and 'ck'. Remind your group of the movements they have to make if they hear words with these sounds. Read your story out loud to your group. Watch out for those children who do the wrong movement.
3. Try to think of movements for other consonant clusters, for example, 'skip' for 'sk'. Learn your new movements with a partner.

HOP, SKIP AND JUMP

OBJECTIVE: to discriminate and identify initial and final consonant clusters in words
LEARNING LINK: auditory, visual
ORGANISATION: small groups
RESOURCES: prepare a list of words as follows: 'hop', 'wink', 'skip', 'jump', 'mend', 'hat', 'cat', 'flat', 'pat', 'bran', 'glad', 'sip', 'ant', 'blue', clearly displayed

WHAT TO DO

● Choose someone to read aloud the words on the list, one at a time.
● Hop if a word has no consonant clusters; skip if a word starts with a consonant cluster; jump if a word ends with a consonant cluster.
● Children who do the wrong action are out.
● The winner is the last child in the game.

NOW TRY THIS

Speed up the game to make it harder. See how quickly children react to each word. How many children can the reader catch out?

CATCH AND RHYME

OBJECTIVE: to identify families of rhyming CVC words
LEARNING LINK: auditory
ORGANISATION: whole class; small groups
RESOURCES: a large soft ball

WHAT TO DO

● Stand in a circle around the teacher.
● The teacher throws the ball to a child and says a CVC word, for example, *hat*.
● The child tries to catch the ball and say a word that rhymes with 'hat'.
● Repeat the game. Practise as many rhyming words as you can, for example, 'hot' and 'dot' or 'pin' and 'bin'.

NOW TRY THIS

Play the game again, using words with a long vowel sound, such as 'snake'.

PLOT THE WORD

OBJECTIVES: to link sounds to letters; to spell and write words primarily using phonics
LEARNING LINK: tactile, visual
ORGANISATION: whole class
RESOURCES: large letter cards (lower case), for each child; select children to stand holding their letters cards in a random order (ensure that their letters cards will spell out a word, when ordered correctly)

WHAT TO DO

● The teacher will choose some children to stand at the front of the class holding their letter cards.
● Look at the letters that the children are holding.
● If you are chosen, try to move the children so that their letter cards spell out a word.
● Now read the word you have spelled.

NOW TRY THIS

Make this game harder by spelling out a short sentence using a human alphabet line.

BEANBAG SPELLING GAME

OBJECTIVE: to spell common irregular words
LEARNING LINK: tactile, visual
ORGANISATION: whole class, standing in a circle
RESOURCES: a beanbag; A4-sized letter cards placed at the feet of each child in the circle

WHAT TO DO

● One child stands in the middle of the circle with beanbag.
● The teacher whispers in the child's ear a word for them to spell.
● The child throws the beanbag to the children who are standing behind the letters that spell out the word.

NOW TRY THIS

1. This time, the teacher throws the beanbag around the circle. Try to guess the word that is spelled out.
2. Extend the above game by throwing the beanbag around the circle to spell a short message. Throw the beanbag in the air to show the start of a new word.

BOUNCE AND COUNT LETTERS

OBJECTIVE: to recognise the critical features of words: length
LEARNING LINK: auditory, tactile, visual
ORGANISATION: small groups, standing in circles
RESOURCES: a hall or playground; a medium-sized ball, for each group

WHAT TO DO

● Choose a child to stand in the middle of the circle, holding the ball.
● This child says a word and throws the ball to someone else in the group.
● Bounce the ball to match the number of letters in the word.
● Award one point for every correct answer.
● The winner is the child with the most points.

NOW TRY THIS

1. This time the child bouncing the ball must also say the letters as the ball is bounced. Award a point for every correct answer.
2. Play the game again, but this time, the child bouncing the ball says their surname and then the letters as the ball is bounced. Award one point for every surname spelled correctly.

MIME IT!

OBJECTIVE: to read and spell two-syllable and three-syllable words
LEARNING LINK: visual
ORGANISATION: small groups
RESOURCES: stacks of ten cards, with words that children can mime (make sure words are phonetically decodable, for example, 'animals') for each group

WHAT TO DO
- Choose a card and look at the word on it.
- Take turns to mime the word on your card.
- Ask the others to guess what the word is and then to spell it aloud.
- The child who guesses correctly has the next turn.

NOW TRY THIS
Play this game against the clock. How many words can be guessed and spelled correctly, in three minutes?

SHORT, MEDIUM AND LONG

OBJECTIVE: to discriminate syllables in multi-syllabic words
LEARNING LINK: auditory, visual
ORGANISATION: small groups or whole class
RESOURCES: prepared list of words containing from one to three syllables, as follows: 'house', 'bedroom', 'dinosaur', 'doctor', 'hen', 'chicken', 'crocodile', 'elephant', 'milk', 'bucket', for each group

WHAT TO DO
- The teacher reads out the list of words, one at time.
- After each word, use your arms to show whether the word is long, medium or short.
- For long words of three syllables, stretch your arms wide. For medium words of two syllables, hold your arms closer to your body. For short words of one syllable, hold your hands close together.
- Continue the activity until all the words have been read.

NOW TRY THIS
1. Hold up the correct number of fingers to show how many syllables are in a word.
2. Think of your own words and play this game again. Can you think of any words with three syllables?

BOUNCE AND COUNT SYLLABLES

OBJECTIVE: to discriminate syllables in multi-syllabic words
LEARNING LINK: auditory, tactile, visual
ORGANISATION: small groups, standing in a circle
RESOURCES: a list of words containing up to four syllables, as follows: 'ball', 'dictionary', 'centimetre', 'fork', 'football', 'lemonade', 'leg'; 'restaurant', 'rhinoceros', 'scarecrow', displayed clearly; a medium-sized ball, for each child

WHAT TO DO
- Choose a child to stand in the middle of the circle, holding the ball.
- That child says a word from the list and throws the ball to someone else in the group.
- Bounce the ball to match the number of syllables in the word.
- Award one point for every correct answer.
- The winner is the child with the most points.

NOW TRY THIS
Try and think of more words that contain four syllables. Bounce the ball as you say the word, to show the number of syllable beats. Possible words: 'invitation', 'caterpillar', 'television'.

MIME AND SPELL

OBJECTIVE: to investigate spellings of verbs with 'ing' endings
LEARNING LINK: auditory, visual
ORGANISATION: whole class
RESOURCES: prepare a list of present tense verbs ending 'ing', before the activity

WHAT TO DO
- One child mimes a verb, for example, 'jumping'.
- Put up your hand if you know the verb.
- The teacher chooses one child to guess and spell the verb. Remember to spell each verb with the 'ing' ending!
- If the child is right, they mime the next verb.

NOW TRY THIS
1. Practise spelling verbs with 'ed' (past tense) endings.
2. Practise spelling verbs with 'ing' and 'ed' endings against the clock. How many verbs can you spell in one minute?

SKIP THROUGH THE ALPHABET

OBJECTIVE: to order letters alphabetically
LEARNING LINK: auditory
ORGANISATION: small groups
RESOURCES: a skipping rope, for each group

WHAT TO DO

● Two children each hold one end of the rope and start to turn it.
● The rest of the group take turns to run into the rope and skip.
● Starting from 'a', each child skips five times, saying five letters of the alphabet as they do so, in the right order.
● The child skipping from the letter 'u' onwards must say six letters.
● If a child makes a mistake they must jump out of the rope. The next child then starts from the last correct letter.

NOW TRY THIS

Play the game again, but this time the children must skip while saying the alphabet backwards for five letters. The child skipping from f–a must skip six times while saying the remaining six letters.

ORDER, ORDER!

OBJECTIVE: to order words alphabetically
LEARNING LINK: tactile; visual
ORGANISATION: whole class
RESOURCES: sets of five word cards (each set of words should be simple and should begin with the same letter, for example, Set 1 – five words all beginning with 'b', Set 2 – five words all beginning with 'd'); you will need to select five children to stand and hold each card within each set

WHAT TO DO

● Look at the cards the children are holding. The words all begin with the same letter.
● Look at the second letter of each word to help you place all five words (and the children) in alphabetical order. You may need to move on to looking at the third letter!
● As a class, check that the words have been ordered correctly.

NOW TRY THIS

Put the groups of words in alphabetical order.

SEQUENCING THE DAYS OF THE WEEK

OBJECTIVE: to sequence days of the week
LEARNING LINK: tactile, visual
ORGANISATION: groups of seven
RESOURCES: seven word cards showing the days of the week, for each group

WHAT TO DO

● Each child chooses a word card and holds it.
● Say the day and its number in the week, for example, *Monday – Day 1*.
● Now, practise putting the days in order, by lining up all the children in the group.

NOW TRY THIS

Choose a child to place all the word cards in the right order. Does everyone agree with the choices made? Suggest changes if needed.

SORTING OUT THE WEEK

OBJECTIVE: to spell the days of the week
LEARNING LINK: tactile, visual
ORGANISATION: whole class, split into seven small groups
RESOURCES: large letter cards (make sure there is a sufficient number of cards to spell one of the days of the week) for each group

WHAT TO DO

● Look at the letter cards.
● Sort the letters, with your group, to spell a day of the week.
● At the end of the session, hold up your cards in the right order to show the others the day that you have spelled.
● Now order the groups to show the correct sequence for the days of the week.

NOW TRY THIS

1. Repeat the activity for months of the year.
2. Select one child to place the children holding the cards for the months of the year into groups of the four seasons: spring, summer, autumn, winter. How quickly can they do this?

WHAT A WEEK!

OBJECTIVE: to spell the days of the week
LEARNING LINK: visual
ORGANISATION: small groups
RESOURCES: seven cards, each showing a different day of the week, for each group

WHAT TO DO
● Choose a card and read the day of the week, silently. Don't show your group your card!
● Mime an activity that your class always does on that day, for example, for Wednesday, you could mime taking part in games during a PE lesson.
● The other children guess the day and one member of the group spells it aloud. If correct, that person takes the next turn to mime a day.

NOW TRY THIS
Shuffle the day cards and place them face down on the table. Turn the cards over, one at a time, to show the days of the week in the right order. If the sequence is broken, the game begins again until the week has been correctly sequenced.

WHICH MONTH?

OBJECTIVE: to spell the months of the year
LEARNING LINK: visual
ORGANISATION: whole class
RESOURCES: 12 large cards each showing a different month of the year

WHAT TO DO
● Twelve children stand in a line, holding a month card.
● Reorder these children so that the month cards are in the right order.
● The children now turn their backs, so that their cards cannot be seen.
● Try to spell each month in turn from memory.
● If you are correct the child holding the card turns round to face the front.
● Play the game until all the months have been correctly spelled.

NOW TRY THIS
Shuffle the month cards and hand them out randomly. Arrange the cards into the four seasons.

SKIPPING GAME

OBJECTIVE: to sequence and spell months of the year
LEARNING LINK: auditory
ORGANISATION: small groups
RESOURCES: a skipping rope, for each group

WHAT TO DO
● Two children each hold one end of the rope and start to turn it.
● The rest of the group take turns to run into the rope, skip once and say the name of a month. Remember to say the months in the right order!
● Keep skipping until all the months of the year have been said.
● Repeat the activity, but this time, keep skipping until you have spelled out your month of the year.

NOW TRY THIS
Say and spell the days of the week in the right order.

LISTEN AND SPRINT

OBJECTIVE: to investigate words that sound the same but are spelled differently: homophones
LEARNING LINK: auditory, visual
ORGANISATION: whole class, in the hall
RESOURCES: large cards placed around a hall as follows: 'grate', 'great', 'hare', 'hair', 'fair', 'fare', 'bow', 'bough', 'sow', 'sew'

WHAT TO DO
● The teacher says a word and then uses it in a sentence, for example, *Fare: The girl had to pay a fare to ride on the bus.*
● Run to the card that shows the right spelling.
● If you run to the wrong card, you are out.
● Continue playing the game until all the words have been used.

NOW TRY THIS
1. Spell a hidden word correctly, by listening to a short sentence that contains it.
2. The teacher will ask you to think of some more words that sound the same but are spelled differently. Now play the game again, using the new words. The adult will choose a child to be the caller. The caller must remember to use each word in a sentence when they call it out.

HOPSCOTCH SPELLING GAME

OBJECTIVE: to spell numbers zero to nine
LEARNING LINK: auditory, tactile, visual
ORGANISATION: small groups
RESOURCES: a hopscotch grid; a beanbag, for each group

WHAT TO DO

● Take turns to throw the beanbag on to a number in the grid. Each time it is your turn, aim for the counter to land in number order (counting on from zero to nine).
● If the beanbag lands on the correct number, hop to that number square.
● Stand still on the square and spell the number word, before returning to the start line again.
● Repeat until you have completed the hopscotch game and spelled all the numbers correctly.
● If at any point you spell a number incorrectly, miss a turn.

NOW TRY THIS

Play hopscotch using numbers 10–19.

ALPHABET JUMP

OBJECTIVE: to read and write own name
LEARNING LINK: auditory
ORGANISATION: small groups or whole class, standing in a circle
RESOURCES: none

WHAT TO DO

● Say the whole alphabet slowly.
● Listen for the letters in your name.
● When you say a letter that is in your name, jump as many times as the letter appears.

NOW TRY THIS

Play the game again, but this time, say the alphabet backwards!

CATCH AND SPELL

OBJECTIVE: to spell high and medium frequency words with increasing confidence
LEARNING LINK: auditory, tactile
ORGANISATION: whole class, standing in a circle
RESOURCES: a beanbag

WHAT TO DO

● One child chooses a word from the weekly spelling list.
● The teacher then throws a beanbag to a child.
● If you catch the beanbag, say the first letter of the word.
● Throw the beanbag to another child who says the second letter.
● Play the game until the whole word has been correctly spelled.

NOW TRY THIS

Practise spelling as many words as you can against the clock. How many words can you spell in three minutes?

MARCH AND SPELL

OBJECTIVE: to spell the name of the school
LEARNING LINK: auditory
ORGANISATION: small groups or whole class
RESOURCES: none

WHAT TO DO

● Stand in a line.
● Now march around the hall to the chant: *2, 4, 6, 8, who do we appreciate…* – spell out the name of your school.
● Remember to march in time and to clap out the letters as you spell the school's name.

NOW TRY THIS

Use the same chant to spell out the names of teachers and some class helpers.

SPELLING SKITTLES

OBJECTIVE: to spell numbers to ten
LEARNING LINK: auditory
ORGANISATION: small groups, in a hall
RESOURCES: a medium-sized ball and ten skittles, for each group

WHAT TO DO

- Stand the skittles a short distance away from you.
- Take turns to roll the ball at the skittles.
- Count out loud how many skittles you knocked down.
- Spell out the number word for the total skittles that you knocked down.
- If you spell out the word correctly you get a point.
- The winner is the person with the most points.

NOW TRY THIS

Use 20 skittles to practise spelling number words to 20.

TEAM SPELL

OBJECTIVE: to spell high and medium frequency words with increasing confidence
LEARNING LINK: auditory
ORGANISATION: whole class, divided into two teams of six
RESOURCES: a hall; one balloon for each team; you will also need teaching assistant(s) to help listen for each team's spelling accuracy

WHAT TO DO

- Stand in a line behind your team leader.
- The leader in each team holds a balloon.
- The teacher says a word from the weekly spelling list.
- The leader spells the word out loud. If correct, the leader runs to the back of the line and passes the balloon forward until it reaches the front person.
- The teacher gives a new word to the front person and the game continues as before.
- If a spelling is incorrect, the whole team can offer suggestions.
- The winning team is the first one to complete all the words correctly.

NOW TRY THIS

Make this game harder by spelling the words backwards!

BEANBAGS AND BUCKETS

OBJECTIVE: to spell CVC, high and medium frequency words, with increasing confidence
LEARNING LINK: auditory, visual
ORGANISATION: small groups, in the hall
RESOURCES: a beanbag and a set of three buckets, for each group (each set of three buckets should contain word cards for three-, four- and five-letter words respectively, for example, Bucket 1: top, tap, hit, cut, hen; Bucket 2: fast, wind, jump, shop, chin; Bucket 3: stand, blink, catch, today, other)

WHAT TO DO

- Place the buckets at a short distance from you. Make sure that the bucket with three-letter words is nearer than the buckets with four- and five-letter words.
- Take turns to try and throw the beanbag into a bucket.
- If your beanbag lands in a bucket, the teacher takes a card from that bucket and reads the word to you.
- Spell the word.
- If you are right, you get a point.
- Play the game until the end of the session.
- The winner is the person with the most points.

NOW TRY THIS

1. Play the game with four, five and six-letter words.
2. Make this game even harder by playing against the clock. How many points can each player score in two minutes, one minute or thirty seconds? Who can win the most points in the shortest time?

Which word?

sock/sack

hand/pond

dent/tent

bank/sink

ramp/lamp

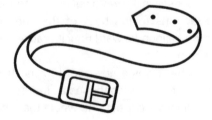

bolt/belt

■ SCHOLASTIC
www.scholastic.co.uk

DAILY SPELLING TEASERS FOR AGES 5–7

Name _____   Date _____

Picture clue crossword

1		2	

Across

1.

3.

5.

Down

1.

2.

4.

PHOTOCOPIABLE

57

Name _____ Date _____

Match the sound

■ Read the story below.
■ Listen for the words that have the '**air**' sound.
■ Now circle all the words that have the '**air**' sound.

Once upon a time, there was a little bear. His name was Blair. But poor Blair had no hair. Clare, his owner, had an idea. She made him a wig to wear. The wig was made of fair hair. Blair put on the wig. He looked in the mirror but the wig gave him a scare.

"I don't dare wear this wig," he said. "I shall hide it over there, behind that chair!"

I found [   ] words with the sound '**air**'.

SCHOLASTIC
www.scholastic.co.uk

PHOTOCOPIABLE

DAILY SPELLING TEASERS **FOR AGES 5–7**

Name _____   Date _____

Crocodile alphabet

■SCHOLASTIC
www.scholastic.co.uk

Write the word

All change

Tessellating tangles

ing

ass

ag

ant

ar

ap

cl ock

gl ad

br ick

pl um

st amp

sl ip

an

um

own

fl ay

ack

ide

Name _____ Date _____

Word maze

▪ Trace over the lines from the top words to the words at the bottom.

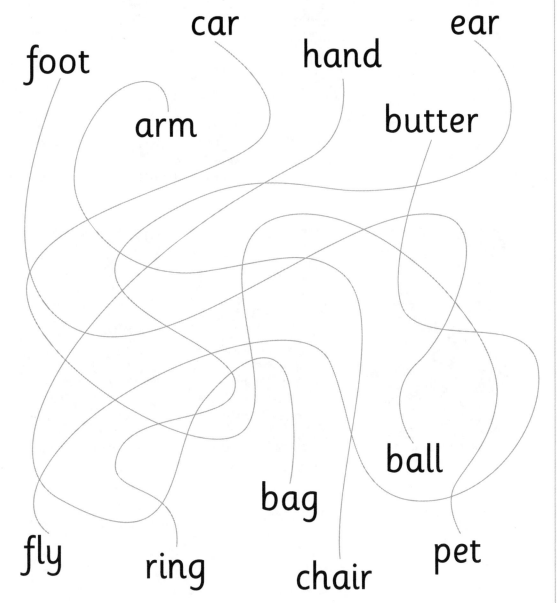

▪ Join the words together and write the new words in the space below.

_____ butterfly _____   _____   _____

_____   _____   _____

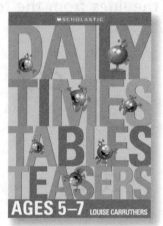